# Five Tragic Hours

# Five Tragic Hours

## THE BATTLE OF FRANKLIN

*James Lee McDonough*

*Thomas L. Connelly*

The University of Tennessee Press

Knoxville

*Frontispiece*: The Confederate Cemetery where more than 1,400 soldiers are
buried. *Photograph by Rudy E. Sanders.*

Clothbound editions of University of Tennessee Press
books are printed on paper designed for an effective
life of at least 300 years, and binding materials
are chosen for strength and durability.

*Library of Congress Cataloging in Publication Data*

McDonough, James L., 1934–
Five tragic hours.
Incudes bibliographical references and index.
1. Franklin (Tenn.), Battle of, 1864. I. Connelly,
Thomas Lawrence. II. Title.
E477.52.M35 1983          973.7'37          83-3449
ISBN 0-87049-396-5
ISBN 0-87049-397-3 (pbk.)

# CONTENTS

# ILLUSTRATIONS

## MAPS

## PHOTOGRAPHS

# FOREWORD

## by James Lee McDonough

MY EARLIEST MEMORY of Franklin goes back to about 1940, when I was a very small boy. My parents took me with them to visit their friends Claude and May Williams, who lived in the house at 908 West Main (Carter's Creek Pike). I remember the fine home—Mapledene it is called—but even more I remember a beautiful lawn where a number of couples gathered in the pleasant early evening to eat and talk. There, in the yard, I was on the bloody Franklin battleground for, I think, the first time. Although I did not then know such facts, I was only a short distance inside the Federal defensive line which crossed the Carter's Creek Pike and bent back northwestward toward the Harpeth River. Directly across the street from Mapledene was the impressive antebellum residence where once lived a fifteen-year-old lad who watched from the boughs of an oak tree in his front yard as the Confederate army deployed for battle in 1864. My first memories of the battlefield, thanks to my parents and their friends, were good ones. It would be a number of years, of course, before the small boy began to realize what had actually happened on that ground nearly a century before.

Another vivid memory of Franklin dates from a few years later, in my teen years, and is associated with the old, no longer extant, Willow Plunge swimming pool. I lived in Nashville, but liking Willow Plunge better than most of the pools close to home, I went there frequently. At some point in those high school and college days, I realized the pool was located where heavy fighting had taken place in the battle of Franklin. One day, in my wet swimming suit, I walked a few hundred yards to the southeast to see the Confederate cemetery. Not wishing to demonstrate any lack of respect for the dead, and in the idealism of youth, I worried just a bit about my atire, but quickly rationalized that even if scantily clothed I was properly motivated. That first visit to the cemetery, on a hot summer day, was deeply moving. I still find it moving when I occasionally go there today, although I would suggest a visit in the winter when the swimming pool of the immediately adjacent Carnton Club is closed and the weather is too cold for tennis balls to bounce properly on the courts beside the cemetery. Winter is more appropriate anyway, since the battle was fought on the last day of November.

A few more years passed and I was selecting a topic for a Ph.D. dissertation in history. I choose the Civil War career of Major General John M. Schofield, in part (and really it was a large part of the reason) because the subject presented a chance to study the Middle Tennessee campaign of 1864 in some depth. Geographically, the Middle Tennessee area is one of the most beautiful in the country, while the campaign is one of the war's most intriguing military studies, climaxed by the sanguinary battle at Franklin. Considering my background and interests, it was a good subject— like my first memories of Franklin.

Still more years went by. I wrote a book about Shiloh, another about Stones River. From time to time I thought about Franklin as a possibility for yet another book and even collected some more material about the subject. And, fortunately, I came to realize that Professor Thomas L. Connelly also had a deep interest in the battle of Franklin. Writing this book with Tom Connelly has been a very special pleasure. If anyone knows more about, or has more understanding of, the Confederacy's western army, the Army of Tennessee, than Tom, I have no idea who that person might be. Even though working hard to complete the manuscript, always I enjoyed my association with him, benefitted from his broad knowledge of the war generally, and was buoyed up by a close camaraderie as we combined forces to produce a book that is important to both of us.


Nashville, Tennessee
*January 1983*

# FOREWORD

## by Thomas L. Connelly

WHERE did my fascination with the Army of Tennessee begin? Such words are often trite, but this book is indeed a labor of love. I grew up in Mother Earth, the rich limestone basin of Middle Tennessee. The region is a spiritual place, and such a comment has nothing to do with the extensive network of religious institutions in Nashville.

It is spiritual because the dark, rich earth around Nashville, along streams such as Brown's Creek or the Harpeth River, embodies a co-mingled feeling of all that was and is the South. As a child of the 1940s I grew into adolescence along the first battleline of General John Hood's army when the remnants of the force destroyed at Franklin moved to Nashville. The first battle line the Confederates established was not far from my home in the old Melrose district. Even then, the saga of the Franklin-Nashville campaign was a special topic for the ruminations of young boys resting on a summer lawn near the Franklin Pike. Down the pike was the Caldwell mansion, Longview, which remains there still. Our version of the legend of the brick archway in the hillside was that the place served as a mystical escapeway into a cave for slaves or army deserters. In effect, it was a springhouse.

The clear spring waters flowed through the valley of Brown's Creek when I was twelve years old and moved out beyond Battery Lane to the region just below the Overton Hills. More than ever, the presence of the Civil War became a reality. Granny White Pike, which ran nearby, was an aged road even before General John Bell Hood's army appeared in 1864. My family's home now stood on the second Confederate battleline. General W.W. Loring's infantry were positioned along the rock wall that formed the north boundary of our property. Off to the west, just across Granny White Pike, Shy's Hill loomed above the valley.

On December 16, 1864, the waves of blue infantry surged

against the hill and General Hood's thin line collapsed. Today Shy's Hill is crowned with fine houses. As a boy, however, I climbed it many times when it was still deserted. The hill and much of the land around it remained as it had been in 1864. On the slopes, I occasionally found relics of the Army of Tennessee which had washed out of the rich soil—the brass facing of a pocket watch, bullets, and other treasures.

Hood's defeated army streamed back through Franklin, where the end of a once powerful Army of Tennessee had come already on November 30, 1864. In terms of the number of Confederate casualties within such a brief time—little more than five hours—Franklin was the South's darkest day. It gave credence to the theories expounded by Grady McWhiney and Perry Jamieson in *Attack and Die: Civil War Military Tactics and the Southern Heritage* that elements within the Southern soul compelled Confederate officers to bleed their armies to death in suicidal frontal assaults.

Yet Franklin's field, like some others of the Army of Tennessee, bore no national military park or splendid monument. One had to search out the memories of the battle. There was the charming Carter House, where young Captain Tod Carter perished on his own back lawn during the battle. As a youth I swam in the old Willow Plunge swimming pool, long since departed. Just up the lane was the beautiful Confederate cemetery where 1,500 men slept, many in unknown graves. Nearby was Carnton, the McGavock mansion, where several of the Confederate generals killed in the battle were laid out on the lower gallery.

The battle of Franklin—indeed, the saga of the Army of Tennessee—has been to me one of those things very real and personal. The story of what occurred on that Indian summer afternoon in 1864 deserves to be told. It is a privilege to join forces with the eminent battle historian James McDonough to tell the story of the Franklin tragedy.

UNIVERSITY OF SOUTH CAROLINA
*January 1983*

# ACKNOWLEDGMENTS

ALTHOUGH no attempt is made here to list all who have contributed to this book, the authors are grateful for the valuable assistance provided by the staffs of many libraries and archives at various times during the past two decades. Without such help this book could not have been written. Also, we are aware of the influence of many historians who have offered sage advice and given encouragement both in our research and writing.

Particularly we would like to acknowledge Grady McWhiney of the University of Alabama and Herman Hattaway of the University of Missouri in Kansas City, who read the manuscript and shared their comments with us. Too, we want to recognize the staff of the Tennessee State Library and Archives which has so often rendered valuable assistance in our work; the members of the Carter House Association, who were most cooperative upon several occasions; Mr. Wade Bobo of Franklin, who made available several source materials from his fine collection; the Louisiana State University Press for granting permission to reprint two maps from Thomas L. Connelly, *Autumn of Glory: The Army of Tennessee, 1862–1865*; Mr. Rudy E. Sanders of Nashville, whose photographic work has contributed much toward making this book attractive; and, finally, we wish to thank everyone associated with the University of Tennessee Press who has worked to produce this volume.

# Five Tragic Hours

# 1 /

# *Dreams of Glory*

H<small>E STOOD</small> on the high slope of Winstead Hill on an Indian summer day in November 1864. Young General John Bell Hood, age thirty-three, was old before his time. In 1861 the shy, six-feet-two-inches-tall Kentuckian had been the idol of Richmond belles. Now he hobbled with a crutch, to support the stump of his amputated leg, caused by a wound at Chickamauga. Gettysburg had not been kind, either. Hood's limp, useless arm hung by his side.

Below him on the slopes of Winstead and Breezy hills, two corps of the Army of Tennessee awaited. In a few moments, Hood would give the signal for the advance. Bands would play and regimental flags would stir in the balmy afternoon air. The corps would lurch forward across the bluegrass plain toward the village of Franklin, Tennessee. The Union army led by General John McAllister Schofield was there, where artillery bristled through the strong earthworks fronted by abatis. Shortly after 4 P.M. on the afternoon of November 30, 1864, the Confederates rushed forward against the Franklin trenches.

For the attackers it would be the worst five hours in Civil War history. Some 1,750 Southern troops would be slaughtered at Franklin—more killed in action than were lost by General George McClellan's massive Federal army in the entire Seven Days campaign around Richmond, or by General Joseph Hooker's army, stylized as the "finest on the planet," at Chancellorsville. Another 5,500 men were wounded or captured. Six generals were killed and a half dozen others wounded or captured.

★ ★ ★

[ 3

Where did it begin, this senseless tragedy of the war's last days, when events had been determined already by massive columns of bluecoated soldiers and mountains of war supplies? Certainly it went back to July 1864, when President Jefferson Davis appointed young General John Bell Hood to command the Army of Tennessee. Davis was disgusted with the strategy of retreat employed by General Joseph Johnston during the long campaign from Dalton to Atlanta in May-July 1864. John Bell Hood came from Virginia with the reputation of being an aggressive fighter.

How fast young Hood had risen in the Confederate army! The Kentuckian had advanced from a captain in 1861 to a division commander by 1862, and was a prominent figure in social life when he visited Richmond. On one such occasion, Hood met the vivacious Sally Preston, popularly known as "Buck," and promptly fell in love. Her reputation for netting suitors was no secret in Richmond, and the amorous Hood pursued her with the same passions he displayed on the battlefield.

By late 1863, Hood's ardor for "Buck" Preston had not diminished, but his mystique had been dampened by the loss of a leg and the presence of a useless arm. He yearned to return to the battlefield, to repeat the same aggressive tactics that had won him fame in Virginia. Jefferson Davis gave him the opportunity at Atlanta. By mid-September 1864, Atlanta was gone and the Army of Tennessee was wrecked.

John Bell Hood's combative tactics had taken a heavy, frightful toll on the Army of Tennessee. It is difficult to determine accurately the losses, suffered in the long campaign from Dalton to Atlanta. It is equally difficult to discern whether the casualties were the responsibility of Hood or of his predecessor, General Joseph Johnston. Political factionalism within the Army of Tennessee made an accurate count hard to obtain. In the latter stages of the war and afterward, Johnston and his supporters maintained that a strong army had been turned over to Hood in July. Hood they said, subsequently wrecked his force in a series of suicidal assaults.

Hood countered by arguing that Johnston's losses from Dalton to Atlanta had been heavy, perhaps as much as 25,000 men.

The truth was somewhere in between. By June 10, 1864, Johnston's rolls of "effective" non-cavalry had listed 50,053 men. By the time of his removal, Johnston's effective infantry and artillery had slipped to 40,850 men. Johnston's medical director indicated that by July 9 the army had lost 9,972 infantry killed or wounded. This figure does not include cavalry losses, troops captured, or deserters. Nor does it include hospital cases of soldiers ill from non-battle causes; by July 1, Confederate hospitals contained almost 11,500 such convalescents. In brief, aside from the non-battle hospital cases, Johnston had lost as many as 12,000 men from causes of battle or desertion.

Hood's losses were much higher in the desperate fighting around Atlanta. The open-field assaults had taken a massive toll. By early September, the Army of Tennessee could muster scarcely 23,000 effective infantry. The number of prisoners and deserters was heavy. The Federals had captured at least 13,000 men. Hood had lost over 12,500 men killed and wounded. The desertion rate was staggering, and thousands of soldiers lay ill in makeshift hospitals. On September 20, John Bell Hood's rolls listed over 62,000 men absent from the army.

Losses in war equipment and foodstuffs signified a shambles. Ordnance, commissary, and quartermaster supplies had been lost by the tons. Gone was the army's entire reserve of gunpowder and ammunition, which had been left behind and destroyed at Atlanta. Some 13,000 rifles and 48 pieces of artillery had been lost to Sherman. Looters plundered commissary warehouses to grab hams, sugar, and a ton of other needed supplies. Railroad equipment was destroyed—some one hundred cars and thirteen locomotives. Destroyed as well were other key installations—the cannon foundry, the Confederate Arsenal, railroad machine works, and other precious industries.

It was a ghost army, something far from the magnificent force that had loomed as such a threat in better days.

★ ★ ★

BUT John Bell Hood yearned still, and dreamed of glory. In late September, President Jefferson Davis arrived at the muddy encampment of Palmetto, Georgia. Morale among the troops was at a low tide. Hood had admitted this to General Braxton Bragg on September 4, speaking of low morale and near mutiny in the ranks. A few days later, General Samuel French, speaking for several unnamed officers, warned the President that the army's morale was bad.

Meanwhile the long dispute between Hood and corps leader General William Hardee cost the army a valuable leader. Hood on September 5 reported to Richmond that Hardee's troops behaved in a "disgraceful" manner at Jonesboro. The previous day, Hood had sent General Braxton Bragg a letter complaining of the conduct of Hardee's and other troops at Jonesboro and accusing the troops of virtual cowardice. Twice later in September, Hood appealed directly to the President to have Hardee removed from command.

The gloomy reports Davis had received were underlined by his reception in Hood's camps, awash with a sea of red clay. The President rode out into the mire to review the thin lines of infantry, only to be greeted by cries demanding the return of General Joseph Johnston to command of the Army of Tennessee.

Meetings with corps leaders were little different. A key conference was held with the senior leader, General William Hardee. Hardee echoed the need for Johnston to be returned to the command. Davis, of course, would have nothing of this. The bitter hatred between the President and Johnston went back over three years—to controversies over the 1861 campaign in Virginia, to the later clash with General George McClellan's force on the peninsula below Richmond, to affairs on the Tennessee and Mississippi fronts in 1863, and to the crowning dispute over Georgia operations in 1864. Instead, Davis suggested another old enemy, but one more palatable, General P.G.T. Beauregard.

One wonders if Davis ever seriously considered Beauregard. Hardee replied that the Creole Beauregard would be acceptable. Also, Hardee insisted that Davis either relieve him from command or replace Hood. Conversations with the two other corps leaders, Tennessean A.P. Stewart and Stephen Lee, brought a similar response. Hood must be relieved, and the suggested replacements were Johnston and Beauregard. The weight of the situation appeared to be on the side of the army's corps leaders. Hood himself had offered to resign.

But Jefferson Davis exhibited his consistent attitude toward the Army of Tennessee, which was almost a contradiction. Davis was a westerner, born in Kentucky and coming to renown in Mississippi. On occasion he had demonstrated great concern for the western front. Two examples bore this out. In 1862, the Confederacy dreamed of recovering Kentucky from the Union. Jefferson Davis was a prime architect of the only joint offensive undertaken

6 ]

by major Southern armies. In August–September 1862, two western armies moved toward the Bluegrass. General Braxton Bragg and Edmund Kirby Smith led their respective forces into Kentucky, while in September, General Robert E. Lee's Army of Northern Virginia invaded Maryland.

The failure of the Kentucky campaign portended disaster for Hood's later aspirations in Georgia. One reason for failure was a lack of unified command. Jefferson Davis's legalistic system of autonomy for an individual army commander negated any genuine cooperation between Bragg and Kirby Smith. Both were departmental commanders, and the President hesitated to name an overall leader for the effort, only hoping for their "cordial co-operation."

When the campaign failed and the unpopularity of Bragg became a public issue in the Confederacy, Davis remained rigid on his belief in territorial autonomy for an army leader. Bragg was not removed from command despite the uproar within the army and elsewhere. Instead, General Joseph Johnston in late November 1862 had been assigned to the command of a vast, ambiguous theater, to cover all territory between the Appalachians and the Mississippi River. Johnston's duties were never defined properly, especially his command authority over individual armies such as those of Bragg in Middle Tennessee and General John C. Pemberton on the Vicksburg front. Certainly many other factors contributed to the collapse of Confederate defenses in the West during July 1863. Clearly the vague nature of the command relationship between Johnston and his army commanders was a factor. Johnston had supervisory authority, but his generals had maintained the same autonomy they held before his arrival in the West.

The loss of Tennessee resulted in the battle of Chickamauga in September 1863, and in a third example of Davis's peculiar handling of matters in the West. There was nothing uncertain about the army's feelings after Bragg's erratic performance at Chickamauga, which netted a battlefield victory but a strategic loss. A secret meeting of Bragg's top generals on October 4 resulted in a petition to Davis for their commander's removal, and in the meantime Davis sent a personal aide, General James Chesnut, to learn the nature of the command turmoil below Chattanooga. Chesnut telegraphed the President to hurry to the army because of the demoralized condition of Bragg's officer corps.

On October 9, 1863, Davis arrived at Bragg's headquarters

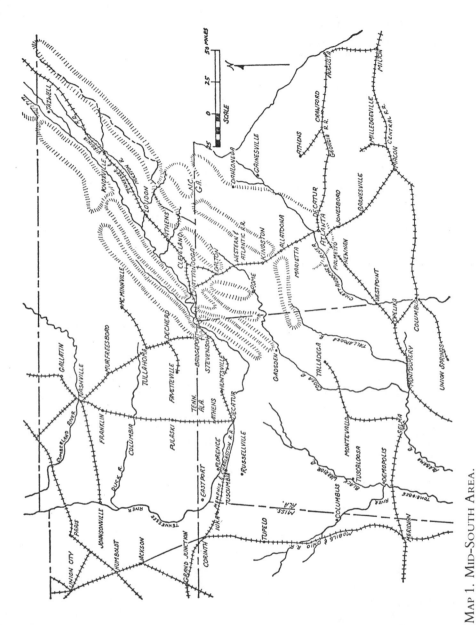

MAP 1. MID-SOUTH AREA.
This map entitled "The Heartland, 1862–1865" is reprinted by permission of Louisiana State University Press from Autumn of Glory by Thomas Connelly, copyright © 1971.

to begin consultations with the commander and major leaders. A subsequent meeting with high officers such as Generals James Longstreet, Simon Bolivar Buckner, and Daniel Harvey Hill—held in Bragg's presence—called for the outright removal of the general.

The responses of President Davis in all three cases were part of the pattern that was again evident after his arrival at Hood's Georgia encampment in 1864. First, the near-mutiny of Bragg's officers at Chickamauga was never understood by Davis. For better or worse, he tended during the Civil War to support his friends and see little that was useful in his enemies. In effect, his decision to back Bragg after Chickamauga dismembered totally the army's command structure. Out of the turmoil at Chickamauga came the loss to the army of valuable officers. General Leonidas Polk, the army's original commander and a veteran corps leader since autumn 1861, was transferred to duties on the Alabama–Mississippi front. Capable Daniel Harvey Hill, a veteran of Lee's campaigns in the East, was removed from command. The splendid cavalry leader General Nathan Bedford Forrest was shuttled off to less important duties in the Mississippi Valley. In fact, of the six wing and corps leaders present on the field at Chickamauga, only two remained after the reorganization in October. Divisions and brigades were rearranged to break down unified anti-Bragg sentiment. For example, the brigade of General John C. Brown, a Bragg critic who later led a division at Franklin, was moved from Harvey Hill's corps to another camp, while regiments of pro-Bragg advocate General W.H.T. Walker were transferred into other units considered less friendly to the commanding general.

In this respect, Davis at Palmetto followed the pattern of past decisions. John Bell Hood had been his trusted confidante in Richmond in 1863, when the one-legged officer was recuperating from his wounds he had received at Gettysburg and Chickamauga. Hood had promised much but had not succeeded; for reasons of friendship or refusal to admit failure, the President now stuck by Hood. On September 28, Davis informed the general he would be sustained. That same day, Hardee was relieved from command and ordered to take command of the lower Atlantic coast. Not one of the men who were now corp leaders of the Army of Tennessee— Generals Benjamin F. Cheatham, A.P. Stewart, or Stephen Lee— had held such a high post before the commencement of the Atlanta campaign.

Another command appointment bespoke a pattern that colored previous upheavals on the western front. Jefferson Davis was a rigid political constitutionalist and military advocate of the Henri Jomini concept of zone command. More than once, his view that autonomous army leaders must protect their own confines had brought the Army of Tennessee to grief. After the failure of the Kentucky campaign, Davis's appointment of General Joseph Johnston to the nebulous post of theater commander had resulted only in confusion. Now at Palmetto, Davis repeated his previous solution to criticism of a commander. This time, instead of removing Hood, he named General P.G.T. Beauregard to lead a new organization stylized as the Military Division of the West, which allegedly oversaw Hood's Army of Tennessee and General Richard Taylor's troops in Alabama, Mississippi, and East Louisiana. The new structure would prove to be a disaster. The Louisianan Beauregard was chosen more as a face-saving device, to silence critics of Hood's performance. From the beginning, his authority of command was vague and weak. On October 2, President Davis explained that while the Creole was supposedly the chief commander on the western front, his authority over an individual army was indeed limited. Beauregard could take charge of an individual army only when "the interests of your command render it expedient."

Obviously Beauregard was confused by this arrangement and sought clarification. Hood's and Taylor's forces comprised two major field armies. When Beauregard visited one, was he supposed to take the actual command or merely issue orders through the commanding general? On November 1, President Davis's reply only added to the confusion. When Beauregard was present in the camp of a particular army, he was to exercise what Davis called "immediate command" but was not "to relieve" the officer commanding the army.

All of this confusion meant, in effect, that General Beauregard had little to do with Hood's planning of the ill-fated Tennessee campaign. The genesis of the disaster at Franklin is confusing because Hood's plans for the Tennessee campaign actually never took shape.

The march from central Georgia into the Middle Tennessee

General John Bell Hood.
[*Dahlgren Collection. Tennessee State Library and Archives (TSLA).*]

country was fraught with constant changes of plans and absolute command turmoil. Initially, the question that faced Hood and his visitor from Richmond on that late September day at Palmetto was what could the Army of Tennessee do in the face of General William Sherman's overwhelming numbers at Atlanta?

Even before Davis arrived at army headquarters, Hood had begun to envision a course of action destined to be changed many times. Obviously nothing would be accomplished by remaining in the encampment below Atlanta. Sherman's powerful Military Division of the Mississippi could only grow stronger through the supply of men and munitions along the central corridor rail line from Louisville via Nashville and Chattanooga to Atlanta. By early September, the Army of Tennessee's intelligence indicated that Sherman was preparing for a forward move into the heart of the Alabama manufacturing region. Thus by September 19, Hood had taken his first step, by shifting his base to Palmetto Station, on the West Point line southwest of Atlanta.

Within a few days after executing this movement, Hood revamped his strategy. Here the future aims of the Army of Tennessee began to take shape. Hood intended to move again, this time to the region northwest of Atlanta, in the vicinity of Rome, Georgia. Such a move, the Kentuckian mused, would threaten Sherman's line of supply via Chattanooga and Nashville, and thus would force the Yankees to move out of Atlanta for a fight. John Bell Hood lived in a world of broken dreams, and he envisioned that his weak army might contest Sherman on a field north of the Chattahoochee. If Sherman spurned the contest and moved southward, Hood would pursue and attack the Federals from the rear.

Jefferson Davis's arrival at Palmetto on September 25 provoked the development of a third design. Now Hood would not only cross the Chattahoochee, but he would move northeastward until he seized the vital Western and Atlantic Railroad to Chattanooga. If Sherman moved against the Confederates and appeared to have great strength, Hood would withdraw into the Allegheny Plateau region near Gadsden, Alabama. If Sherman turned back and aimed for a port in the Deep South, Hood would follow. Such was the plan by September 27.

By the end of the first week in October, intelligence indicated that the latest revision of strategy was working. Already by October 2, Hood's army had seized the Western and Atlantic

Railroad north of Atlanta, demolished the line at several points, and captured Yankee garrisons at Big Shanty and Acworth. Within three days, intelligence reported that Hood's intent to draw Sherman northward from Atlanta was succeeding. By October 5, Sherman's advance units had reached the old battlegrounds around Kennesaw Mountain.

What followed was a series of tangled changes of plan which indicated one of two matters—if not both. Either Hood had no real plan, or already he had intended to violate the agreement made with Jefferson Davis in the Palmetto conference. In that meeting, Hood had assured Davis that whatever the course of the army's operations in northern Georgia, the state would not be abandoned to Sherman. If Sherman failed to pursue and moved toward the Atlantic or Gulf coasts, Hood would pursue.

By October 8, Hood had begun to depart from this concept. He moved the Army of Tennessee off Sherman's supply route on the Western and Atlantic Railroad. Now Hood's position was at Cedartown, Georgia, seventy miles northwest of Atlanta on the Alabama border, and he reported yet another concept of his intentions to General Braxton Bragg in Richmond. He had abandoned the idea of drawing Sherman directly northward from Atlanta and giving battle. Instead, the new strategy involved operations in northeastern Alabama. Hood would operate from a supply base at Gadsden, Alabama. He would march the army to vital crossing points on the Tennessee River west of Chattanooga, at Stevenson and Bridgeport, Alabama. Hood would cross the river, destroy Sherman's communications and depots at those vital points, and then confront the enemy somewhere in northern Georgia.

By the next day, Hood had a different version. His appointed superior, Beauregard, arrived at Hood's headquarters at Cave Spring, northwest of Cedartown. Obviously, Beauregard did not understand what Hood intended to do. The version he received from the Kentuckian was not what Hood had told the government on the previous day. Nothing was mentioned about Hood's ambitions to move to the Tennessee River. Instead, Hood told Beauregard he would operate on Sherman's communications north of Atlanta, give battle if pursued, and follow Sherman back to Atlanta if the Federals withdrew.

At first Hood's actions were in accordance with what was told to Beauregard. Between October 10 and 13, the army swung eastward against the Western and Atlantic Railroad, destroying miles of track and capturing 1,000 garrison troops. Certainly by now Hood was in excellent position to fight Sherman if he so desired. Confederate intelligence indicated that Sherman was indeed in pursuit along the rail line from Atlanta via Kennesaw with only 40,000 troops, having left an entire corps in Atlanta. By now, Hood's army was north of the Oostanaula River, in the Resaca-Dalton region, which was protected by outlying ridges of the Allegheny Mountain fastness of northwest Georgia. If Hood intended to fight Sherman, now was the time.

Hood instead moved away from Sherman's path and struck westward to Lafayette, Georgia, just below the old battleground of Chickamauga. Here, beneath Pigeon Mountain, Hood planned his dreams of glory. Georgia would be abandoned to the Federals. The old vision held by Confederates of marching to the Ohio River loomed again. Desperate to recoup something of his past glorious war image, Hood envisioned a bold crossing of the Tennessee River, followed by a march on Nashville and the invasion of Kentucky. Once at the Ohio River, perhaps Hood would even move through the Cumberland Mountains eastward to threaten Grant's flank and rear.

There was more to this quixotic plan than a revisal of the Confederate dream to redeem Kentucky. In part it was to become the culmination of Hood's own frustrations and blasted dreams. He was far away from the better times as the handsome cavalier of Lee's Army of Northern Virginia whose courage dazzled the public. Even after the frightful wounds of Gettysburg and Chickamauga, Hood was still a celebrated guest in Richmond social circles. But this, too, had soured. Behind in Richmond was Hood's fiancée Sally Preston and confidant Jefferson Davis. His strivings in battle to impress both had ended in disaster at Atlanta. Hood was no longer the darling of the Confederacy. He was a broken soul, old before his time in body and spirit.

Perhaps as well, the Tennessee campaign was one last irrational act of attempting to duplicate the strategic movements of Hood's idols, Lee and Jackson. Hood's boast in his memoir, *Advance and Retreat*, that he was an advocate of the Lee-Jackson school of war applied as much to strategy as it did to field tactics.

Hood was trying to duplicate the war as he remembered it in better days, when he was a hero on the Virginia front. Hood could remember the bold flanking maneuvers of "Stonewall" Jackson as he marched to join forces with Lee on the peninsula. Another audacious flanking move had taken Jackson's men across central Virginia and onto the field at Second Manassas. Then came Jackson's brilliant flanking march at Chancellorsville.

There seems little doubt that Hood envisioned another such bold move through Tennessee and Kentucky. His new plan for the Tennessee campaign was replete with bold strokes reminiscent of Jackson's brilliance.

The problem was, of course, that Hood was not brilliant. He was no Lee or Jackson and lacked the intellectual capacity to supervise such broad maneuvers. The complicated details of Hood's grand scheme would require expert command coordination, careful logistical support, and prompt, decisive action.

Probably not even a Lee or Jackson could have made Hood's plan work, because it would have strained a military genius to his limits. Hood intended to cross the Tennessee River at Guntersville, Alabama, and then seize the Nashville-Chattanooga Railroad. The Army of Tennessee would move to Nashville and replenish its paltry rations with Union army stores. Hood then would cross the Cumberland River and move into the mountainous region of eastern Kentucky, where he could threaten Cincinnati. If Sherman pursued, there would be a battle. If not, the Confederates might push through the mountain passes into Virginia and attack Grant's rear along the Richmond-Petersburg line.

The difficulties and outright errors in such a plan were so profuse that the scheme would have made a textbook study at West Point. In fact, that was only the beginning of Hood's problem. His senior corps officer, the former superintendent of the Military Academy, had left the Army of Tennessee. Jefferson Davis had chosen to retain Hood over keeping the only veteran corps leader, General William Hardee, who might have alerted Hood to some of his errors.

This was the beginning of Hood's strategic flaws. Lee had succeeded in bold strokes because he had possessed, on most occasions, a well-coordinated command structure, particularly in the era of Generals "Stonewall" Jackson and James Longstreet. Hood's lack of control over his subordinates was demonstrated in the mutinous situation that clouded the Army of Tennessee's hopes in the camps at Palmetto. Many corps leaders were veritable spiritual fathers to their junior officers. This had been true with the late General Leonidas Polk and was accurate as well in Hardee's case. His sterling division commander, General Patrick Cleburne—the army's finest—was on the verge of offering his resignation after Hardee was replaced. So now Hood would march into Tennessee with two separate, difficult problems with his lieutenants. Hardee's replacement, General Benjamin F. Cheatham, was an absolute novice at maintaining such authority. The other corps leaders, Generals A.P. Stewart and Stephen Lee, were veterans of the Atlanta battles but possessed scant prior experience in such positions. Added to this woe was the problem of shabby morale among Hood's generals.

Careful attention to details of supply would also be essential for success of these grandiose operations. First, a shift of operations from the Alabama-Georgia border to the Tennessee River would require a drastic change in Hood's base of supply. This would necessitate the use of the decrepit Memphis and Charleston Railroad eastward from Corinth, Mississippi. One sector, over thirty miles in length, had been abandoned and was covered with underbrush.

Even had a first-class rail line been available, subsequent problems for such an invasion were gigantic. Hood's transportation system was in poor condition. Gambler that he was, Hood counted upon the seizure of Nashville to replenish his meager stores. Even if Nashville had been captured and wagons were abundant, how much food and material could they carry into the desolate mountain region of eastern Kentucky during the hard winter of 1864–1865?

Finally, any grand strategic move of the style exhibited by Lee and Jackson required firm, decisive action. Despite his battlefield reputation for aggressive behavior, Hood as a strategist dealt in visions clouded often by indecision and contradictions. No sooner had Hood announced his scheme to the government in dispatches of October 19–20, than he began a long, twisting set of changes in plan. Guntersville did not suit him as a crossing point. Hood's later explanation was that he lacked sufficient cavalry, since theater commander P.G.T. Beauregard had insisted that General Joseph Wheeler's corps remain in Georgia to confront Sherman. Save for General W.H. "Red" Jackson's two brigades, Hood would have no troopers. It had been decided that General Nathan Bedford Forrest's cavalry would be substituted for Wheeler.

Hood's conduct of matters in regard to Forrest was typical of the haphazard nature of his planning for such a campaign. At some point in a meeting between Hood and Beauregard at Gadsden, Alabama, on the night of October 21, it was decided that Forrest's command was to replace Wheeler's. No one apparently knew that Forrest's troopers on October 16 had crossed the Tennessee River on a West Tennessee raid, which took them about a hundred miles west of Hood's destination at Nashville. Hood argued later in his memoir that he changed plans on the night of October 22 after receiving intelligence that Forrest was in West Tennessee. Hood never explained how he mysteriously received such convenient information that night; Forrest was not even ordered to join Hood's column until four days later. And the Forrest explanation does not jibe with Hood's excuse to Beauregard that he did not cross at Guntersville because the area was too heavily guarded.

This was only one element in a pattern of confusion that colored Hood's curious movements across northern Alabama. The next crossing point was westward at Decatur, but the riverfront garrison there appeared too strong to invest. Courtland, twenty miles westward and some five miles south of the river, was the next destination, but Hood changed his mind again. By October 31, Hood finally reached his destined crossing at Tuscumbia, Alabama. It was almost one hundred miles west of the planned crossing at Guntersville. So far, Hood's northward march into Kentucky had been a westward move across Alabama, almost to the Mississippi border.

No one was more puzzled by this than General William Sherman. By October 21, Sherman's advance had reached Gaylesville, Alabama, near the Georgia border, and the general expected Hood to give battle nearby. When Hood first had abandoned his encampments below Atlanta, Sherman had assumed the Confederate were bound for Middle Tennessee. On September 28, General George Thomas had been ordered to Nashville to concentrate reserve forces in Middle Tennessee. By October 3, it appeared that Sherman had been wrong and that Hood's real destination was on the Western and Atlantic Railroad in northern Georgia. Thus Sherman moved northward through Marietta, leaving only a single corps in Atlanta.

Hood's constant shifts of position befuddled Sherman. In early October he complained to one subordinate, "I can not guess his movements as I could those of Johnston, who was a sensible man and only did sensible things." By October 26, after pursuing Hood into Alabama, Sherman made his decision. Whatever the erratic Southerner's course, the Federal army would play the game no longer, and the March to the Sea began to take course. Sherman would leave Hood to Thomas's gathering forces in Middle Tennessee and to reinforcements being sent from Georgia. By October 29, Sherman had ordered the Fourth and Twenty-third corps, under Generals David Stanley and John Schofield, to join Thomas at Nashville.

Far to the west, General John Bell Hood on November 21 moved northeast from the Tennessee River. Early storms of snow and sleet, intermingled with rain, turned roads into mudholes or sheets of ice. What lay ahead Hood did not know. Despite his later declarations of knowledge of growing Yankee strength in Middle Tennessee, he moved forward with only scant information that the Fourth and Twenty-third corps were en route to Nashville.

Hood was in no mood to be concerned with precise details of enemy whereabouts, his supplies of wagons and munitions, and other such matters. His cavalier days in Virginia were far more than a dim memory. Now he marched in one last dream of glory.

# 2 /

# A Gentleman of Fine Address
# and Elegant Manners

Wﾟﾟﾟﾟﾟ ILLIAM TECUMSEH SHERMAN was now famous, and about
to become more so. The lean, red-haired, forty-four-year-
old Ohioan with the grizzled, short-cropped beard need never recall
again those newspaper reports early in the war that he was insane.
He had captured Atlanta. General Henry W. Halleck called the
campaign the most brilliant of the war, and Charles Francis Adams
was ranking Sherman with Napoleon and Frederick the Great,
while the praise from newspapers, telegrams, and letters kept pouring in

And now Sherman planned a bolder stroke, something that
had been in his mind a long time. Even months earlier, at the
opening of the spring campaign, Sherman had been asked what he
would do after capturing Atlanta and reportedly replied: "Salt
water. Salt water." Meditating on the possibility of marching into
the interior of Georgia, he began to correspond with General Grant
about his future operations in early September. Sherman realized
that Grant, since becoming general-in-chief of the armies of the
United States with responsibility for the strategic direction of the
war, was the only person he really had to convince in order to get
what he desired. At every chance Sherman pursued the subject. On
September 20, he wrote Grant: "If you can whip Lee, and I can

march to the Atlantic, I think Uncle Abe will give us twenty days leave of absence to see the young folks."

On October 1, Sherman asked Grant, "Why would it not do for me to leave Tennessee to the force which Thomas has and the reserves soon to come to Nashville and for me to destroy Atlanta and then march across Georgia to Savannah and Charleston, breaking roads and doing irreparable damage." For several weeks Grant and Sherman exchanged telegrams about the proposal and considered various aspects of the strategic situation. On October 11, Sherman wrote that he "would infinitely prefer to . . . move through Georgia, smashing things to the sea."

Grant worried about preparing a coastal base to supply the army, but Sherman replied that his troops would need no supplies, and no base. They would take what they required from the countryside. "I can make the march and make Georgia howl!" said Sherman. Grant was also concerned that Sherman might be "bushwhacked by all the old men, little boys, and such railroad guards as are still left at home." Sherman, however, intended to be plenty strong, planning, as he worded it, to take only "the best fighting material" on his march. The matter was considered by Lincoln, Secretary of War Edwin M. Stanton, and Halleck, as well as Grant. The President was very concerned, but willing to accept Grant's decision.

After weeks of Sherman's pleadings, Grant's earlier fears for Sherman's safety and success subsided. Sherman got what he wanted. Grant advised Lincoln that he considered the proposed march to be sound and telegraphed Sherman that his plan was approved and that he had the "confidence and support of the government" and might "go on as you propose." General George H. Thomas, at Nashville in command of the Department of the Cumberland, was to oppose Hood's advance should he turn back into Tennessee instead of following Sherman.

Undoubtedly, General Thomas, born in Virginia and graduted from West Point in 1840, twelfth in a class of forty-two, was one of the best corps commanders in the Union army. With experience in the Second Seminole War, garrison and frontier duty, the Mexican War, and as an artillery and cavalry instructor at the Point, Thomas had been an army man all his adult life. A severe wound in the face from an arrow only accentuated the fact. When at the secession of Virginia Thomas remained loyal to the Union, his family was so deeply incensed that thereafter his three sisters, at the mention of his name, would reportedly forthrightly announce, "We have no brother." Having fought at such places as Mill Springs or Logan's Cross Roads, Perryville, and Stones River—where he is said to have stoically remarked: "This army does not retreat"— Thomas had never failed in an operation, and as a defensive fighter was probably unsurpassed in either army.

Thomas's greatest moment as a military commander had come at Chickamauga. In the heavy and decisive fighting on the last day of that battle, the Confederates penetrated the Federal line, driving the troops south of Thomas in disorder, along with two corps commanders and the army commander, General William S. Rosecrans. Thomas, however, was still in position to protect the line of retreat to Chattanooga. Although his line was bent back severely, Thomas and about half of the Yankee army continued to hold strategic Snodgrass Hill throughout the afternoon, finally retiring to Chattanooga. At West Point, Thomas had been known as "Old Tom" while a cadet, and "Slow Trot" as an instructor; but after the fight of September 20, 1863, Thomas was known as "the Rock of Chickamauga." Six feet tall and weighing about two hundred pounds, Thomas is described in the *Dictionary of American Biography* as "studious in his habits, deliberate but decided in action, and fastidious to the point of exasperation."

After the fall of Atlanta, General Thomas had favored a campaign south from that city, with his own Army of the Cumberland, which had composed about two-thirds of Sherman's total force in the advance from Chattanooga. But he was opposed to Sherman's plan of marching to the Atlantic coast while Hood was still moving, undefeated, along the Tennessee River. Now that Sherman had Grant's approval for the march, he wrote to Thomas on October 20, arguing that simply to pursue Hood would wear out his army. "I know I am right," Sherman stated. "I think Hood will follow me, at least with his cavalry. . . . If, however, he turns on you, you must act defensively on the line of the Tennessee."

Thomas certainly possessed ample strength at his command to handle the situation, if he could bring all the troops together rapidly. In Nashville he already had some 8,000 to 10,000 soldiers under arms, plus about that many more employees in the quartermaster's department who were available to man the fortifications about the city in case of attack. Also, there were various detach-

ments that could be marshalled at Nashville. There would be James
B. Steedman's 5,000 men at Chattanooga; Lovell H. Rousseau's
5,000 at Murfreesboro; Gordon Granger's 4,000 at Decatur; and a
number of other smaller garrisons—Spring Hill for instnce, with
1,200 to 1,500 men. The two divisions under General Andrew
Jackson Smith, numbering about 14,000, were ordered to return
from Missouri; and Sherman sent the Fourth Corps, under General
David S. Stanley, numbering 12,000, and the Twenty-third Corps,
under General John M. Schofield, numbering 10,000, back to Tennessee to further strengthen Thomas's forces. Including a cavalry
command of some 10,000, being assembled in the Tennessee capital, Thomas would have more than 70,000 men available.

Nevertheless, when Hood began to cross the Tennessee
River, a movement Sherman had thought improbable, Sherman
was irritated; and Grant and Thomas were alarmed. Thomas did
feel confident, however, that with Stanley's and Schofield's troops
added to those already at hand, and if Smith was hurried forward
from Missouri, he would be able to drive Hood back. Sherman did
not think that Hood was in any condition to march on Nashville,
but if he did, Sherman also thought that Thomas would have
sufficient time to concentrate his forces and repel him. Thus Sherman marched out of Atlanta "to ruin Georgia," as he phrased it,
"and bring up at the sea-coast." Hood and the Army of Tennessee
were left for Thomas to stop, if an invasion of Middle Tennessee
should really occur.

While Thomas was in overall command of Union troops
massing in Nashville, actual field command of the forces that
Thomas deployed at Pulaski to delay Hood's advance south of the
Duck River, was exercised by General Schofield. In fact, Schofield
would have the immediate responsibility for directing Federal
troops throughout the ensuing campaign, until the battle of Nashville.

The Federal general taking command at Pulaski was strik-
ingly different from Hood. John McAllister Schofield and John
Bell Hood graduated from West Point the same year, class of 1853,
but there any similarity seemed to end. Even at the academy their

---

General John McAllister Schofield.
[*Brady Collection. National Archives (NA).*]

academic records revealed a marked contrast, Schofield ranking seventh, Hood forty-fourth in a class of fifty-four graduates.

In appearance, temperament, style, and values, the two men were a study in contrasts. Hood was tall and well-proportioned. The thirty-three-year-old Schofield was a little too short and a bit too heavy—even as a young man in his prime—for his general appearance to be arresting, although in later years his graying hair, Burnside whiskers, and military regalia would create a distinguished image. Hood had been dashing, exuding color and charisma; but Schofield seemed "a gentleman of fine address and elegant manners," according to one observer, while another said that Schofield impressed him with the feeling that he was "in the presence of a statesman, rather than a soldier."

A native of Gerry, New York, who spent his teen years in Illinois, Schofield was the kind of man who worked hard, paid attention to details, and kept up with his reports and correspondence—even his memoranda were precise and thorough. Probably he realized that success comes, not always from brilliance, but sometimes by working to avoid mistakes. As commander of the Army of the Ohio in Sherman's summer campaign, Schofield's tactical performance was sound, almost methodical; an indication of his mathematical bearing, also a vindication of his rank as first in the study of infantry tactics among his West Point classmates. Sherman would pay him perhaps the highest compliment he ever received as a military man, describing Schofield as having more ability than General George H. Thomas.

If Hood was aggressive, emotional, romantic, and a dreamer, Schofield was articulate, calm, reflective, and dispassionate, his subtle sense of humor virtually hidden from all except those few who knew him intimately. Schofield, in many ways, was typical of middle-class America on the rise; the ambitious, hardworking, practical achievers who would "make it" to the top of the socio-economic heap in the late nineteenth century, gradually changing, like a chameleon, as and like America changed. (Later, when Schofield became general-in-chief of the United States army, hardly any one seemed to fit the highly industrialized, material-oriented, gaudy culture of the Gilded Age better than he with an evident taste for opulent surroundings, "pulling strings" to make his army inspections in the Pullman "200" coach, the finest sleeper manufactured by the George M. Pullman Company of Chicago.)

In 1864, Schofield was a fitting symbol of the machine-like

efficiency for which the United States army was striving, and which increasingly characterized the Union war effort. The war was being won, not by the colorful, dramatic Sheridans of the Yankee military forces but basically by mass production, mass transportation, and overwhelming numbers. The Federals did not require dash; what really was needed now were methodical men who could manage and calculate. And Schofield—despite General John Pope's remark that Schofield "could stand steadier on the bulge of a barrel than any man who ever wore shoulder straps"— was certainly not a fighter, not in anything like the sense that Hood was; he was essentially an organizer and administrator, for better or worse typifying the northern and midwestern men who were coming to dominate America, politically and economically.

Nevertheless, for all their differences, Hood and Schofield shared one cross in common—the war had been frustrating for both, though the frustration grew out of quite dissimilar experiences. Schofield did see action very early in the war, as an aide-de-camp to General Nathaniel Lyon at the Battle of Wilson's Creek, where a newspaper reporter observed him "ever in the lead, the foremost, coolest soldier in all that bloody fight." But following Wilson's Creek, Schofield had to settle down to humdrum military tasks in Missouri, organizing and disciplining militia, trying to break up and suppress bands of guerrillas, pursuing seemingly phantom Rebel forces, and fighting off an attack of typhoid fever. A highly ambitious man whose career was not keeping pace with his expectations, and in fact seemed stagnated, Schofield manifested some less than admirable traits during this period of the war. He became extremely discouraged, engaged in petty quibbling with his department commander, General Samuel R. Curtis, and at last wrote General-in-Chief Henry W. Halleck, complaining that Curtis "was really the cause of all my troubles" and begging Halleck to transfer him to some other command where he would not have to encounter such "sloth" and "imbecility." By 1864, Schofield probably was still capable of dealing with people whom he did not like, or who stood in the way of his ambition, in the same underhanded vein. There would be allegations that Schofield intrigued to replace Thomas as Federal commander at Nashville; that he sent reports to Grant criticizing Thomas for not moving more quickly to the attack. And there is considerable circumstantial evidence to support this charge.

For a while in 1863 Schofield had been elevated to command

the Department of Missouri, a vast area encompassing Missouri, Kansas, the Indian Territory, and part of Arkansas. However, he had been unable satisfactorily to maintain a middle ground between the struggling political factions, and President Lincoln transferred him to command of the Department of the Ohio, establishing headquarters in Knoxville, Tennessee. For a long time Schofield had been politicking through General Halleck, Senator John Henderson, and others, in an effort to gain an assignment in a major military campaign. After the extensive reorganization that brought Grant to the head of a central command system for the Union war effort, Schofield had gotten what he wanted. In the spring of 1864 he became one of Sherman's army commanders for the campaign into the heart of Georgia. While Schofield's Army of the Ohio was really no more than a small corps in numbers, it was designated an army for organizational and administrative purposes. From Schofield's point of view—and most important—he then had a responsible command position under a capable general in one of the significant campaigns of the war.

Yet, as promising as the Atlanta campaign seemed at its inception, the long trek did not bring Schofield the opportunity to distinguish himself. Although occasionally Schofield was assigned to carry out a flanking movement against the tough Confederate defenders commanded by Joseph E. Johnston, usually the flanking marches were performed by the Army of the Tennessee, led by James B. McPherson, another of Schofield's West Point classmates. The campaign never resulted in a situation where a major battle was waged by the whole army and, while Schofield acquitted himself well enough, any glory he may have hoped to gain from the campaign had eluded him.

Schofield would finally gain a measure of fame in this Middle Tennessee campaign of late 1864. Ironically, much of the publicity could not have been welcome to the general. While Schofield professed to consider the campaign an excellent demonstration of tactical skill on his part, and proudly lectured about it in later years, in the twentieth century the Spring Hill–Franklin campaign would be frequently cited for gross blundering on Schofield's part, from which he escaped only by a combination of incredible luck and the even greater bungling of Hood. The American Civil War was never to bring the ambitious Schofield the fame and glory he so desperately sought—and thought he deserved.

Nevertheless, the years following the war would be far kinder to Schofield than to Hood. In the years to come, Schofield would serve as military director of Reconstruction in Virginia, as secretary of war, as commander of the Divisions of the Pacific, the Missouri, and the Atlantic, as superintendent of the U.S. Military Academy at West Point, and, finally, as commanding general of the army from 1888 to 1895, the year of his retirement. With increasing maturity and success, he would seem less petty, more mellow, and would, in fact, come to demonstrate an open-mindedness and realistic good sense that eventually combined to make him, as a military man, seem wise beyond the age in which he lived. And unlike many of the officers whose careers reached a climax in the Civil War, Schofield would not regard the techniques of the Union army as sacred and unchangeable. While military men in Europe and America would be obsessed with a kind of Darwinian militarism, glorifying war, Schofield would publicly deplore war as at best nothing but a sometimes necessary evil. All this was far in the future, of course, when Schofield assumed command of the Federal forces assembling at Pulaski, Tennessee, on the morning of November 14, 1864.

The general purport of Schofield's instructions from Thomas was that he should delay Hood's advance as much as possible in order to gain time for the concentration of all available forces and the arrival of General Andrew Jackson Smith's command from Missouri. He was not supposed to try to defeat Hood by himself. General David S. Stanley was already present with the Fourth Corps. With the arrival of a portion of Schofield's own Twenty-third Corps, the total Yankee infantry would number about 22,000. Also at hand was a small section of cavalry, approximately 3,500, under General Edward Hatch. Hood would be advancing with about 40,000 soldiers, but, of course, these numbers would not remain constant during the ensuing campaign. Schofield's force would increase as he retired toward Nashville, picking up garrison troops, and more cavalry when General James H. Wilson joined up as the new cavalry leader. Confederate numbers, on the other hand, would decrease somewhat, both because of the allurement of home and family and because of casualties; the cavalry, particularly, covering the Confederate advance, suffered. Also, the harsh weather hit the poorly equipped Rebels worse than the Yankees. By the time of the legendary Spring Hill episode and the awful battle at

Franklin, the Confederates actually engaged were not many more, if any, than the Federals.

Schofield had just arrived at Pulaski when Stanley greeted him with disturbing news, pointing out the isolated position that the Union troops occupied. Stanley was an Ohioan whom Schofield had known since their days together at the Point, where Stanley had graduated in the class of 1852, a year ahead of Schofield. A veteran of the Indian wars and border distrubances on the Kansas frontier, Stanley, too, first saw Civil War action at Wilson's Creek, afterward spending the entire war in the western theater. For a while he had commanded the cavalry corps of the Army of the Cumberland and then led an infantry division during the Atlanta campaign, where he had been wounded at Jonesboro, but recovered in ample time to resume command of a corps at Pulaski. There is reason to believe that feelings between Schofield and Stanley might not have been ideal. Years afterward, in his memoirs, General Stanley would write of Schofield that he could "pick [Schofield's] chapter on Jonesboro to pieces," but did "not think it worthwhile." And of the campaign upon which the two were embarking, Stanley would record that "all said in Schofield's book as to his foreseeing and providing to meet the events as they unfolded, is the merest bosh." He "assumes a grand superiority and wisdom, in each case at variance with the facts, and appropriates circumstances entirely accidental and the run of luck in our favor as a result of his wise foresight."

Stanley was a man of some ability, and indeed there was reason for concern about the Pulaski situation. The town was thirty miles south of Columbia and the crossings of Duck River, from which ran the turnpike and the railroad to Nashville, which was about forty-five miles north of Columbia. To the west of Pulaski lay the town of Lawrenceburg, with a direct road to Columbia through Mount Pleasant. The superior Confederate force might elect to race for the bridges at Columbia, which were guarded by less than 800 men, and block the Yankees' line of retreat to Nashville. Making the Federal position worse was the small cavalry command. Hatch's force would be facing the troops of the aggressive veteran Forrest, numbering 7,000 or more, who could probably screen any Rebel movement effectively. Accurate information regarding Confederate intentions would be difficult to obtain.

Upon hearing Stanley's objections to the position, Schofield, as yet unfamiliar with the terrain, halted General Jacob D. Cox's division four miles north of Pulaski, there situated to cover a road from Lawrenceburg until Schofield had time to consider his alternatives. Soon aware of the danger of his exposed locale, Schofield sent a dispatch to Thomas at Nashville on Sunday afternoon, November 20, suggesting that he move his main force to Lynnville, which was halfway to Columbia. The message well summarized the Federal situation; it was, in fact, almost prophetic: "If Hood advances, whether his design be to strike this place or Columbia," Schofield theorized, "he must move via Lawrenceburg, on account of the difficulty of crossing Shoal Creek. Under cover of his cavalry he can probably reach Lawrenceburg without our knowledge and move his forces a day's march from that point toward Columbia before we could learn his designs, and thus reach that point ahead of us; or," continued the Federal commander, "he might move upon this place, and, while demonstrating against it, throw his forces onto the pike north of us, and thus cut us off from Columbia and from our reinforcements. Lynnville would be free from these objections as a point of concentration for our forces."

Thomas replied that there was little hope of Smith's troops arriving from Missouri before Friday. While he hoped that Pulaski might be held until then, he agreed that Schofield must withdraw to Columbia if Hood attempted to cut him off from the crossings of Duck River. Although Schofield clearly believed that it would be wise to leave Pulaski, he said, in deference to Thomas, that he would "consider the move more maturely before deciding." Also, he mistakenly thought that Hood, due to the heavy rains in recent days that made the road difficult to travel, could not reach the vicinity of Pulaski any earlier than Tuesday "at best."

Feeling that he had sufficient time to make his dispositions, and also thinking that it would "be well to avoid the appearance of retreating when it is not necessary," Schofield started Cox's division back to Lynnville on the morning of November 22, and planned to move Stanley's forces back the next day. Stanley marched about two o'clock in the afternoon of November 23, bivouacking at Lynnville late that night, as Cox, meanwhile, had moved to within seven miles of Columbia where he called a halt for the night. But, on this day, Hood's advance nearly kept pace with Schofield's.

Hood's army had been moving forward since the morning

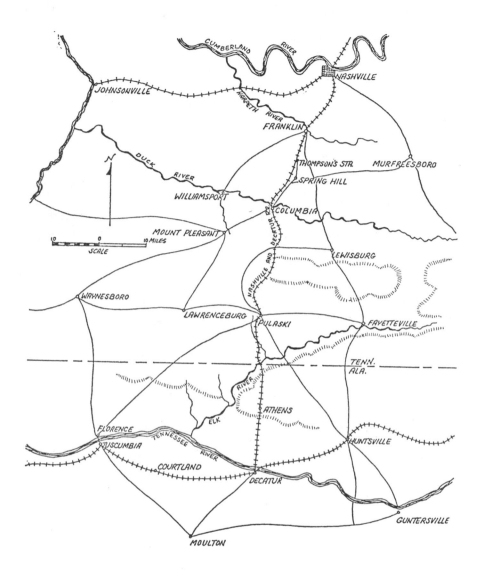

MAP 2. HOOD'S APPROACH TO NASHVILLE, AUTUMN 1864.
Reprinted by permission of Louisiana State University Press
from Autumn of Glory by Thomas Connelly, copyright ©
1971.

of November 21, a day that opened with an unseasonably early blast of snow and sleet and closed with a hard freeze. The three corps advanced along separate roads, all in a generally northern direction. Leaving Florence, General Benjamin F. Cheatham's corps was on the left of the army, moving on the road to Waynesboro. General Alexander P. Stewart's corps was on the army's right, marching on the road to Lawrenceburg, while General Stephen D. Lee's corps advanced on the country roads between the two main pikes.

Operating in front of the infantry was the cavalry command, led by the tough, aggressive, forty-three-year-old General Nathan Bedford Forrest. The legendary six-foot, one-inch cavalryman from Bedford County, Tennessee, whom Sherman had recently described as "that devil Forrest," was having no trouble, according to General Hood, in driving the Federal cavalry, in brisk actions, "from one position to another." Forrest himself reported that for three days there was "almost constant skirmishing," in which the advancing Confederates "drove the enemy in every encounter."

The left column of the Rebel cavalry, under James R. Chalmers, with Forrest present, was moving toward Columbia, through Henryville and Mount Pleasant, pushing Horace Capron's Federal cavalry brigade before it. Schofield, camping at Lynnville with Stanley, received an alarming message near midnight of November 23 from General Thomas H. Ruger in Columbia, revealing that Capron had been fighting the Confederate cavalry all day and had been driven back to Mount Pleasant. Now alive to the closeness of the enemy and the peril of the situation, Schofield at 1 A.M. on November 24 dispatched an urgent message to General Cox, leading his advance infantry. "All information indicates that Hood is nearer Columbia tonight than I am," said Schofield, who instructed Cox to "march at once to or near Columbia and hold the enemy in check as far out as practicable long enough for Stanley to get in. . . . The question is to concentrate the entire force at Columbia in time."

Schofield had depended too much upon his conviction that the bad weather would slow Hood's march. He did not have sufficient cavalry to inform him accurately of Confederate movements. Hood was pressing Schofield more closely than the Federal commander had anticipated. Still, Hood's infantry was not as near to Columbia as Schofield apparently thought, but certainly there was good reason to be worried about Forrest's cavalry. General

Cox received Schofield's dispatch about 4 A.M. on November 24, and before daylight he was marching for Columbia.

Thirty-six-year-old Jacob Dolson Cox was just the man for the job. Born in Canada of U.S. parents, he grew up in New York and Ohio, graduated from Oberlin, and became a lawyer and state senator before the war began. Entering the Union army, Cox distinguished himself at South Mountain, commanded a corps on the bloodiest single day of the war at Antietam, and led a division in the Atlanta campaign. Following the war he would be governor of Ohio, secretary of the interior, president of the Wabash Railroad, and serve in the United States House of Representatives, as well as write a two-volume memoir of the Civil War and a history entitled *Atlanta and the March to the Sea—Franklin and Nashville*. An admirer would later call him a universal genius, "world famous as an authority on microscopy and cathedral architecture, literator, politician, artist, soldier—everything."

Adam J. Weaver, a soldier in the One Hundred and Fourth Ohio Infantry, wrote about the general in a letter to "Charlotte," a woman he would marry after the war. "You will please excuse me if I praise General Cox of our Third Division frequently in my letters to you, but I am unable to help myself," said Weaver. "He is the best general here. He looks like a lawyer or maybe a preacher. Talks like a professor of higher learning. He is a self made soldier of sheer force of character and sense of duty. Conducts the war business with dignity and dispatch."

Cox had a high energy level—as his many activities and accomplishments would seem to imply—and on this day, November 24, he moved rapidly and decisively to gain control of the road into Columbia upon which Forrest was advancing. About seven-thirty, when two miles from town, he arrived at a crossroad leading westward to the Mount Pleasant pike. Cox sent his wagon trains on into Columbia and turned his command off to the left, striking for that pike, which he had learned was about a mile away.

Firing could be heard in the distance. Reaching the Mount Pleasant Pike at an intersection approximately three miles from Columbia, Cox was just in time to interpose his infantry, moving up at the double-quick gait, between General Forrest's cavalry and

---

General Nathan Bedford Forrest.

[*TSLA.*]

the brigade of Colonel Capron, which was being driven back rapidly. Cox's infantry soon checked the advance of the enemy cavalry, and a line was formed behind Bigby Creek. Schofield, at the head of Stanley's column, rode into Columbia about ten o'clock. As fast as the Union troops arrived, Schofield set them to throwing up earthworks that would cover the approaches to the town from the south, while the wagon trains were sent across the river.

During the next two days, while Hood's infantry labored along on the rough roads below Mount Pleasant, Schofield entrenched a semicircular line of works running from the river above to the river below the town. Forrest's cavalry had Columbia invested throughout this period, maintaining an irritating fire against the Federal lines. After making an examination of the ground, Schofield was convinced that Hood would try to turn his position. Thus he informed General Thomas that he would prepare an interior and shorter line that could be held by about 7,000 men. When necessary, Schofield could retire to this line and send the greater part of his force north of the Duck River.

As the new interior Federal line was occupied, Cox's division retained its original advanced position across the Mount Pleasant Pike. All the while the Confederates kept up a heavy artillery action and some sharp skirmishing. But General Thomas J. Wood—still trying to live down blame laid on him for defeat at Chickamauga where, due to a misunderstanding at army headquarters, he moved his division out of line, in obedience to orders, and left a gap through which the Rebels charged—noted that by two o'clock on the afternoon of November 25 the Confederates had deployed only a single infantry division, doing most of the skirmishing with dismounted cavalry. It was clear to Wood that Hood was merely demonstrating, intending to make a major move elsewhere.

By the evening of November 27, Hood's infantry had deployed in front of Columbia, having relieved Forrest's cavalry, which, that morning, had been sent farther out to picket and scout for crossings along Duck River. During the night Schofield evacuated the town, moving to the north side of the Duck. With the crossing completed, he burned the bridges and took position to carry out Thomas's instructions to delay Hood's northward advance until the troop concentration at Nashville could be completed.

34  ]

The night of November 27 was bitterly cold, and snow was falling as Hood's infantry and cavalry corps commanders were summoned to his headquarters at Beechlawn, Mrs. Amos Warfield's house, three miles south of Columbia on the east side of the Pulaski Pike. There he outlined a striking plan. Forrest's cavalry would move up the Duck River the following day, while the rest of the infantry was still arriving, and seize several fords within a space of twelve miles. Then Forrest could drive back any Federal cavalry to permit Hood to lay a pontoon bridge at Davis' Ford.

On November 29, Hood, with Cheatham's and Stewart's corps, would cross the river and march on the Davis' Ford Road to Spring Hill, twelve miles north of Columbia on the main pike to Nashville. One of Lee's divisions would accompany Hood. The other two would remain at Columbia with the army's artillery and trains, and would demonstrate heavily to hold Schofield on the north bank opposite Columbia.

While Hood was planning his strategy, Cheatham's corps, which would lead the advance to Spring Hill, had camped between the Mount Pleasant and Pulaski Pikes, near Ashwood Hall, the residence of Colonel Andrew Polk. The mansion stood only a few hundred yards from St. John's Church, which was located at the intersection of a road to the little community of Ashwood. General Patrick Ronayne Cleburne, the Irish-born commander of one of Cheatham's divisions, noted the beauty of the small church in its quiet grove and the adjacent cemetery. To his aide, Cleburne remarked that it was almost worth dying, "to be buried in such a beautiful spot."

# 3 /

# The Spring Hill

# Affair

S PRING HILL is a sleepy little town, set in a pleasant, comfortable, agrarian community about thirty miles south of Nashville, approximately halfway between Columbia and Franklin. If the Civil War soldiers could see the village today, they probably would think that it has hardly changed since November 1864.

The population is still small. The rolling hills of bluegrass pastureland present a soothing, pleasing panorama. And the great mansions built by a few of the wealthy citizens still stand, among them the fine house, with extensive mahogany interiors, where General Richard S. Ewell, one of Lee's corps commanders at Gettysburg, spent his last years; the majestic Martin Cheairs mansion with its Greek columns in which, one day in the spring of 1863, Dr. George B. Peters shot and killed Confederate General Earl Van Dorn; and the red brick, four-columned home of the William McKissacks. It was Jessie Helen McKissack, a beautiful brunette, who married Dr. Peters and whose widely rumored trysts with Van Dorn led a jealous husband to assassinate the general.

Actually, there was nothing particularly significant about Spring Hill. A bit of unwelcome notoriety had resulted from the Van Dorn murder, of course. Yet the town generally had been little affected. But now the relentless march of history—its course so often strange—would forever stamp the name *Spring Hill* among the famous legends of the war.

Traditionally the Confederate army at Spring Hill, on November 29, 1864, has been credited with an outstanding opportunity, somehow botched, to trap Schofield's Union force and deal it a mortal blow. What went wrong in the Rebel army has been one of the great mysteries of the conflict. Long after death had silenced the voices of the longest-lived veterans, the perplexing enigma would continue to attract countless students of the war. Explanations of Confederate failure have run the gamut from the providence of the Lord to the work of Federal spies. "God just didn't want 'at war to go on no longer," was the solution given by an old black preacher who had been one of the slaves around the Absalom Thompson house when General Hood spent the night. Some elderly residents of Spring Hill, as well as old veterans, said that Hood was drunk; or that the commander of his lead corps, General Benjamin F. Cheatham, was intoxicated or spending the night with the famous Mrs. Peters—she was in town and her husband was not—or both. There was even the fantastic account of a Federal soldier, J.D. Remington, Company I, Seventy-third Illinois Volunteers, who claimed that "the Confederate generals allowed themselves to be deceived by taking orders from two Federal spies." Remington referred to himself and a cousin who allegedly destroyed Rebel attempts to coordinate effective action by spreading countermanding, confusing, and contradictory orders to various enemy officers.

Bruce Catton presented a typical interpretation of the campaign when he wrote that Schofield allowed Hood to steal a march on him, "and by the afternoon of November 29 had his army in position at Spring Hill, ten miles in Schofield's rear. By everything in the books Hood now had a winning advantage. Schofield had to retreat, his escape route ran right past Hood's front, and one hard blow might obliterate him." The perplexity of the problem is demonstrated by the opposite viewpoint of Stanley Horn, well expressed in *Civil War Times Illustrated*, when he wrote that the Federals at Spring Hill simply "got there first with the most men," and Hood never had much chance to hurt Schofield's army.

What happened at Spring Hill and why will never be completely explained. But we do know that much of the confusion about the whole campaign began with General Hood himself. His long-range objectives were clouded, and he apparently was not certain of his immediate objective either. Dazzled by the memory of "the immortal Jackson," as he fondly described the famous Virginian, and inspired with the opportunity to make one of those "beautiful moves upon the chessboard of war," Hood had laid out a bold plan to execute a flank movement on the Union left. This much is clear. The goal of the flanking march is something else.

Later the move would be depicted (and Hood himself contributed to the distortion by his subsequent claims) as an ingenious march to entrap Schofield at Spring Hill. Hood would place the main body of his army, so it would be alleged, at the little village twelve miles north of Columbia, directly across the main road to Franklin and Nashville, in excellent position to attack the Yankee force as it moved northward. While turning on his West Point classmate would be a possibility, Hood's favored intention may not have been that at all. What he really seemed to desire, based on primary evidence, was to gain the pike in Schofield's rear and outrace the Federals to the Tennessee capital. As snow fell on the night before the fateful march, and the Confederate council of war adjourned, General Hood spoke to Chaplain, later Bishop, Charles Quintard, who recorded in his diary: "Hood detailed to me his plan of taking Nashville and calling for volunteers to storm the key of the works about the city." The next morning, while Confederate soldiers moved through the predawn darkness to cross the Duck River at Davis' Ford, Hood told Quintard that the army would "press forward with all possible speed and . . . would either beat the enemy to Nashville or make them go there double quick." Still again, the chaplain recorded that Hood said "the enemy must give me a fight, or I'll be in Nashville before tomorrow night."

Evidently the Confederate commander knew little about potential Union strength at Nashville. Maybe he even still considered Schofield's troops the only major barrier to capturing the capital—if so, it was indeed a tragic misconception, considering the overwhelming numbers eventually assembled there behind some of the strongest fortifications in America. A determination to plunge straight ahead for the city, outracing Schofield to Nashville, might explain a woeful lack of planning for the Spring Hill event. Hood's corps leaders, Cheatham and Stewart, marched without any specific orders, without most of the army's artillery, and without their

---

General Benjamin Franklin Cheatham.

[*Dahlgren Collection. TSLA.*]

ammunition trains. With dreams of glory, hungering for some kind of triumph, Hood was once more strapped to his saddle as he led the infantry of the Army of Tennessee in person, riding with Cheatham near the head of the flanking column. Stewart's corps followed Cheatham's, reinforced by one of Lee's divisions.

As the lead corps commander, Cheatham's role would be highly important, second only to Hood's, in the success or failure of the movement. A native Nashvillian, descended on the maternal side from James Robertson, founder of the city, the colorful, forty-four-year-old Cheatham was a veteran of both the Mexican War and the California Gold Rush who had returned to Tennessee and participated prominently in the state militia in the years before the war. Cheatham was generally popular with his men. Commissioned a major general shortly before commanding a division at Shiloh, he had been in most of the Army of Tennessee's great battles, earning a reputation as a fierce fighter. Standing five feet, eight or nine inches tall, Cheatham was powerfully built—"stout, rather rough-looking," according to an English visitor in 1863—with light blue eyes, light brown hair, and a heavy moustache. He "presents the appearance of a soldier," according to one of his men, being a "quite commanding figure." Cheatham's physical strength and cursing were legendary. So, too—if the allegations of some are accepted—was his drinking; although it is unlikely that he could so long have retained a high position of command if he was a habitual drunkard. For better or for worse, the coordination of the Rebel movement would depend, primarily, upon Hood and Cheatham.

Both the Confederate crossing of Duck River and the march northward, parallel to the turnpike four miles west, were uncontested, thanks to the spearheading efforts of General Forrest's horse soldiers, who had forced a crossing of the river farther east and taken the Federal cavalry out of the campaign altogether. General James H. Wilson's Union troops were first beaten in an action at Hurt's Corner and then driven back along the Franklin–Lewisburg Pike, which ran roughly parallel to the Columbia–Spring Hill Road. Detaching a brigade to keep up the pressure on the retreating Federals, Forrest turned the rest of his cavalry westward for a strike at the Spring Hill garrison, two regiments numbering perhaps 1,200 to 1,500 men.

Meanwhile, if Hood's plans were a bit vague, it is hardly surprising that Schofield was unsure about Confederate intentions.

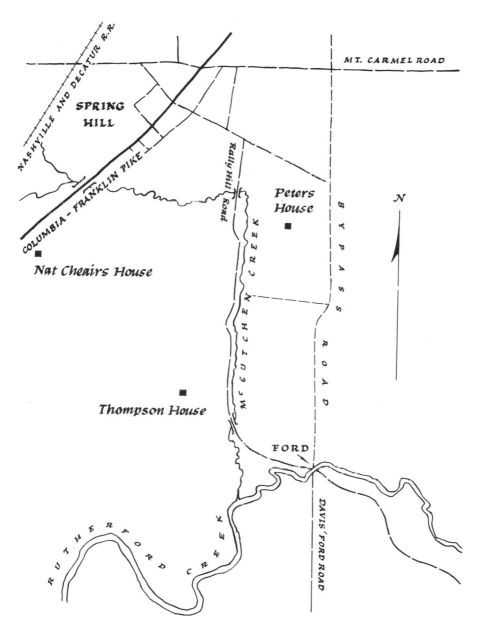

MT. CARMEL ROAD

NASHVILLE AND DECATUR R.R.

SPRING HILL

COLUMBIA – FRANKLIN PIKE

Rally Hill Road

Peters House

McCUTCHEN CREEK

BYPASS ROAD

N

Nat Cheairs House

Thompson House

FORD

DAVIS' FORD ROAD

RUTHERFORD CREEK

MAP 3. SPRING HILL.
  Map prepared by Sharon McDonough.

First, he likely entertained doubts concerning the reliability of his new cavalry commander Wilson. One of the war's "boy wonders," the twenty-seven-year-old had become a major general only five years after graduating from West Point. Actually about five feet, ten inches in height, Wilson's slim frame appeared a trifle taller, and his bearing commanded attention. Never one to be bashful about claiming success, while always careful to minimize his failures, Wilson actually came close to losing an entire division in his first independent operation in Virginia, a fact that Schofield may or may not have known.

Undoubtedly Wilson was a man of considerable ability, but also he was inclined to be somewhat pompous and even self-righteous. His massive conceit led him to later depict both Grant and Thomas as being strangely inert at Missionary Ridge, Wilson taking credit for conceiving the attack that won the battle. Often an unreliable witness, he would write in the same manner about Thomas and Schofield at Nashville, giving the impression that if it had not been for him neither would have attacked on that battle's second day. Although Wilson had just joined Schofield along with 4,000 horsemen, bringing the Federal cavalry almost to a par with the Rebel cavalry, Schofield is certain to have considered Wilson's capabilities to deal with the veteran Forrest as highly questionable. Later, from Franklin, Schofield would dispatch a telegram to Thomas saying, "I do not know where Forrest is. . . . Wilson is entirely unable to cope with him."

Wilson's conduct probably irritated Schofield from the start. Shortly before daybreak of November 29, Schofield received a dispatch from Wilson saying that information from prisoners indicated that the whole of Forrest's cavalry was in his front and that pontoon bridges were being laid over the Duck for the passage of Hood's infantry. Wilson thought Hood was "aiming for Franklin" and advised Schofield to retire northward along the pike with his entire force. Wilson then, instead of regrouping and riding to help secure the infantry's line of retreat, continued to retire toward Franklin. Schofield resented Wilson telling him to "get back to Franklin without delay" as if he were giving the orders.

The Federal commander was not at all convinced that Hood

---

General James Harrison Wilson.

[*Brady Collection. NA.*]

was driving for Franklin or Spring Hill—or any other place along the pike to Nashville. The Confederate movement might be only a feint, intended to cause him to retreat from Columbia and thus leave open the macadamized road to Nashville for the advance of Hood's infantry and artillery. Also, if Hood was actually crossing the river with the greater part of his infantry, he might strike down the right bank to attack the Yankee left flank. This is apparently what Schofield assumed was most probable, particularly after the Confederates opened a heavy artillery fire against the Union lines from Columbia, clearly demonstrating that most of Hood's guns were still in the town.

Thus Schofield made his decision. He would hold on at Columbia, at least for a while. Deploying his men to meet either a Rebel movement on the pike to his rear or a strike down the Duck River against his left flank, Schofield positioned General Nathan Kimball's division east of the pike between Duck River and Rutherford's Creek, supported with General Thomas J. Wood's division, thereby protecting the Federal left flank. General Thomas H. Ruger's division was sent just north of Rutherford's Creek, on the pike about halfway to Spring Hill, ready to move either north or south, while General Stanley continued to Spring Hill with General George D. Wagner's division, the army's train of eight hundred wagons, and most of the artillery. The rest of the Union army, under Cox, stayed in the lines at Columbia. Schofield calculated, or so he later claimed, that if he had to race for Spring Hill he could beat the Confederates, who would be marching farther and on a rougher road.

Somewhat like Wilson in one respect, Schofield, too, was never inclined to shrink from taking credit for making the necessary allocations to meet all contingencies. Still, it took no great wisdom to recognize Spring Hill as a possible Confederate objective. That Schofield would attempt an estimate of the marching time required to cover the distance is only to be expected. The accuracy of his calculation is another matter.

It was a very close affair—probably much more so than Schofield ever anticipated—that unfolded on what several soldiers described as a beautiful fall day. Perhaps the greatest danger for the Federal army came at noon when, if the Yankee infantry had been a few minutes later in arriving, Forrest's troopers might have taken Spring Hill from the two-regiment garrison. General Stanley was riding with the head of Wagner's division, about two miles south of the town, when he was advised by a breathless courier that Forrest's cavalry was galloping toward Spring Hill on the Mt. Carmel Road, only about four miles out.

Responding instantly with "the biggest day's work I ever accomplished for the United States," Stanley brought the infantry into Spring Hill on the double-quick, Colonel Emerson E. Opdycke's leading brigade arriving at about 12:30, in the nick of time to help the garrison defenders stop General Abraham Buford's division of Forrest's troopers from seizing the village. Following the bloody repulse of this initial attack by Forrest's leading division, Stanley hurried to strengthen his position. Parking the wagon train between the turnpike and the railroad, west of town, he deployed Wagner's three brigades, led by Opdycke, General Luther P. Bradley, and Colonel John Q. Lane. Forming a long, semicircular line covering the high ground, the Yankees were positioned, at the farthest point, a third of a mile or so east of Spring Hill, with both flanks withdrawn to cover the pike above and below the village. Opdycke was on the left, protecting the wagons, Bradley in the center, facing east, and Lane on the right, looking south.

Forrest probably did not realize how close he had come to capturing the town. But, by the time Forrest had deployed his cavalry for a direct attack, Stanley had 6,500 or 7,000 infantry on good ground, under cover of a quickly constructed breastwork of rail fences, with thirty-four guns facing south and east in support of the infantry. It was not a bad position. Forrest was surprised to find such strong resistance and, without specific orders, was probably unsure of what to do. If Hood had really intended to seize the pike for the purpose of trapping Schofield, Forrest could have swept around Spring Hill and made a lodgement on the pike to the north. Instead, he wasted some men in assaults on the village until nearly 3 P.M., when his ammunition ran low.

About that time General Hood, riding at the head of the Rebel infantry column, reached the crossing of Rutherford's Creek, two and a half miles southeast of Spring Hill. There the Davis' Ford Road intersected the Rally Hill Road, which led to the town. Without consulting Forrest, and completely ignorant of the strength of Stanley's position, Hood sent forward his leading division under General Patrick R. Cleburne—a division enjoying the distinction of being the hardest-hitting unit in the Army of Tennessee—instructing Cleburne to council with Forrest and then seize the pike. Corps commander Cheatham would await the arrival of General William B. Bate's division, marching after Cleburne, at the crossing and lead it to Cleburne's support. Hood himself would then send forward Cheatham's final division, that of General John C. Brown, when it came up.

Cleburne failed to make personal contact with Forrest and thus knew little, if anything, of Stanley's position. Veering west from the Rally Hill Road toward the Columbia-Franklin Pike, his right brigade soon blundered into the Yankee line southeast of Spring Hill. Cleburne swung his division northward toward the town and, around four o'clock, barely half an hour before sunset, made the first infantry assault on Stanley's position. Tyree H. Bell's dismounted brigade of Forrest's cavalry supported him. Cleburne drove the Federals back from their fence-rail works only to be swept by a galling artillery barrage from three batteries massed on the southern outskirts of the village in anticipation of just such a situation. With Bell's men out of ammunition and Cleburne's infantry disarranged by the attack, the division commander had to fall back and reform before he could assault again. Stanley had seen the regimental flags bearing the full-moon device of Cleburne's division. The Federal general was worried, and he warned Wagner to brace his soldiers for the Rebels' return, probably with substantial reinforcements.

Meanwhile, Hood and Cheatham were working at cross-purposes, the former attempting to seize the pike while the latter planned an assault on Spring Hill. Rapidly the Confederate effort went to pieces as Hood and Cheatham reversed each other's orders (the Federals not needing a spy to do it). First, Cheatham did not personally conduct Bate to the front as Hood had instructed. Thus Bate proceeded north along the Rally Hill Road until he met Hood returning from sending Cleburne forward. The Confederate commander ordered Bate to move west to the pike and then "sweep toward Columbia." About dark, Bate penetrated close to the pike on the Nat Cheairs farm, a mile and a half south of Spring Hill. Just at that moment a Federal division was spotted marching northward toward the town; skirmish firing erupted, and Bate prepared to advance and seize the road but received an order from Cheatham to pull back from the pike. Cheatham instructed Bate to march northeast and form on Cleburne's left flank facing Spring Hill.

The Martin Cheairs House, where Dr. George Peters shot Confederate General Earl Van Dorn.

[*Photograph by Rudy E. Sanders.*]

Bate reported the contact with the Union force—probably Ruger's division, the lead element of Schofield's main body—to his corps commander, but Cheatham apparently was unimpressed, his attention now centered on Stanley's forces at the village. Cheatham had moved to Cleburne's front, learned of his difficulties, and ordered Bate to his support. Then, as Brown's division moved up, Cheatham ordered it to form on Cleburne's right flank. While Cheatham planned a full-scale assault on Spring Hill with his corps, Hood evidently knew little about what was occurring. He did not remain on the field, retiring to his headquarters at the Thompson farm, a couple of miles south of the village.

The Confederate effort continued to deteriorate. Cheatham's attack never got underway. Brown was scheduled to begin the assault on the right, to be followed by Cleburne when he heard Brown's guns, with Bate going forward in coordination with Cleburne. About 5:30, with darkness now totally enshrouding the scene, Brown was in position. However, he delayed the attack because his line was badly outflanked. If he advanced, Brown said, "inevitable disaster" would be the result. Cheatham said he told Brown to throw back his threatened right flank and attack anyway. But Brown claimed he was ordered to wait until Stewart's corps came up and hold himself ready for further orders then. For whatever reason, and presumably some misunderstanding of orders had occurred, Brown never did attack. Consequently, of course, neither did Cleburne or Bate.

More ineptness now foiled both the seizure of the Columbia Pike and the assault on Spring Hill, as Stewart's corps, which had been following Cheatham's at a short distance, was held up just south of Rutherford's Creek by Hood's orders. The reason is a puzzle. Riding to Hood's headquarters to learn why his corps was not being deployed, Stewart was told something that made no sense, only demonstrating, if anything, Hood's almost total ignorance of the situation. Stewart was being held in reserve, said the commander, to pursue any retreating Federals who might try to escape on the Rally Hill Road.

About this time Hood received a note from Governor Isham Harris, indicating that General Brown was outflanked and recommending that Stewart march to Brown's right and seize the road north of Spring Hill. Hood, probably thinking Brown faced westward near the pike, when actually he was hundreds of yards away and angled toward the north, approved the suggestion. He ordered Stewart's corps to march on a road parallel to and east of the Rally Hill Road, a route that would intersect the turnpike north of Spring Hill. It was about six o'clock when Stewart left to begin the movement.

Unfortunately, he got lost. Located an hour or so later on a country road east of Spring Hill by a courier from Hood who directed him to an alignment with Brown's right flank, Stewart realized at once the position would not achieve his original order to get on the pike. Dismayed, he rode back to Hood's headquarters.

Apparently Hood had believed that, once in position, Stewart's line would bend around to the pike north of town. Now, evidently for the first time, he understood the actual situation at Spring Hill, at least in general terms, and discovered that no one had seized the Columbia–Spring Hill Pike. At last, much of the confusion about operations at the village had been cleared up.

Surprisingly, however, Hood did not seem particulary concerned, nor did Stewart and Cheatham. When Stewart reported that his position did not occupy the pike from Spring Hill to Franklin, Hood merely asked if he could spare a brigade to block the road. Contending that his men were tired and hungry, Stewart declined. Hood then told Stewart to go ahead and bivouac his corps for the night. Also Hood told Cheatham, as Cheatham later recalled, that he "had concluded to wait until morning, and directed me to hold my command in readiness to attack at daylight." The Rebel commander did turn to Forrest, asking if he could place a brigade on the pike. Two of Forrest's divisions were completely out of ammunition. The third had only a small supply captured from the Federals. While Forrest vowed to do what he could, this was obviously a move with little promise of success, in spite of Hood's alleged optimistic remarks to General Bate. According to Bate, when he told Hood about the conflicting orders he had received earlier in the evening, the general said, "It makes no difference now, or it is all right, anyhow, for General Forrest, as you see, has just left, and informed me that he holds the turnpike with a portion of his forces north of Spring Hill, and will stop the enemy if he tries to pass toward Franklin, and so in the morning we will have a surrender without a fight. We can sleep quietly tonight."

Why did Hood not order either Cheatham or Stewart to advance and take possession of the pike? Surely they could have occupied it either north or south of the town. And General Edward Johnson's division of Lee's corps had finally come up behind Stewart and taken position near Cheatham's left flank, actually camping in the area initially occupied by Bate near the Cheairs home. Why not order Johnson's division to take possession of the pike?

Apparently Hood held another important misconception on November 29. Almost totally lacking in knowledge of the region's terrain, he probably assumed that Schofield would have considerable difficulty in reaching Spring Hill. Based on his own long, hard march—even recognizing that Schofield had a shorter route—Hood likely thought that Schofield would not reach the village that evening, and certainly could not go farther north. Probably Hood was confident, judging from his lack of action, that the morning of November 30 would find the main Yankee force still between Spring Hill and Columbia. His belief would have been reinforced by the sound of Lee's artillery at Columbia, heard periodically during the afternoon and evening, presumably still pounding the Union lines. Also, he had no report that Schofield had begun a rearward movement. Hood actually boasted that night to another officer that morning would find the Confederates between Schofield and Franklin.

Thus Hood did not go personally, or even send a staff officer, to observe conditions on the pike. This may be partially explained as an outgrowth of his overconfidence regarding the strategy with which he supposedly had handicapped Schofield. Still, he could have taken some steps to insure that the Federals would not bypass him during the night, and because nothing should be taken for granted in war, his failure to do so seems strange until one remembers the general's physical condition. By midnight of November 29, Hood probably was in no shape to make military decisions. The stump of his leg likely was irritated by the long ride over rough roads. There is some evidence that he was generally exhausted. Especially if he took any liquor or a drug to relax and ease the pain, his desire to believe that everything was working out well could have been obsessive.

Fully consistent with such an interpretation was Hood's rather blasé reaction when a barefoot private came to the farmhouse headquarters some time after midnight, reporting that he had seen Union infantry columns moving on the turnpike in large numbers. Hood only roused himself long enough to tell his adjutant, Major

The Absalom Thompson House, Hood's command post on the night
of November 29, 1864.

[*Photograph by Rudy E. Sanders.*]

A.P. Mason, to instruct General Cheatham "to advance a line of skirmishers" and "confuse" the Yankees by firing into their column. Immediately Hood went back to sleep.

Like Hood, Cheatham did not bother to investigate the matter for himself, but passed the word to General Edward Johnson. The division commander did examine the pike, finding the road empty. Possibly he had encountered a gap between segments of the Federal army on the march; possibly some of the Yankees could have filed off the pike on a road to their left, mentioned by General Bate in his After Action Report, and come into Spring Hill by a less direct country road; also a posssibility, since the time is very uncertain and conceivably might have been long past midnight (at least one participant so remembered the hour), is that the last of the Federals had just passed. In any case, Johnson soon returned to his headquarters, while Schofield's troops continued to trek north in spite of the Confederates sleeping nearby in the fields to the east. Unquestionably, in some places, the Rebels were very close to the tramping Union army; a lieutenant in gray later wrote that "Federal soldiers came out to our fires to light their pipes and were captured."

Incidentally, the contradictions and confusions of later accounts by participants are nowhere better illustrated than in the conflicting stories of General Cheatham and Governor Isham Harris regarding the note that Hood ordered Major Mason to send to Cheatham. While Cheatham wrote that he received a note "about midnight" by courier from Mason, Harris recorded that the next day Mason drew him aside and revealed that he had never sent Cheatham the order—the order Cheatham said he received. "I fell asleep again before writing it," said the major, as he explained that General Cheatham was not to blame for failing to make a night attack. Did Mason send the note and simply forget that he had done so? Obviously, there is no means now of unraveling the truth.

It had been about three o'clock in the afternoon before Schofield became satisfied that he would not be attacked in force at Columbia, that, instead, Hood was marching to seize the pike somewhere to the north. The Federal commander then led Ruger's two brigades in a rapid march to Spring Hill, leaving staff officers to give orders to the other division commanders to follow shortly. Schofield rode into Spring Hill about seven o'clock.

Once in the town he conferred with Stanley, learning that no help could be expected from Wilson's cavalry and, worse, that some of Forrest's troopers had been seen at Thompson's Station, about three miles to the north on the road to Franklin. Fearing that the enemy had occupied a favorable position dominating the pike, Schofield led Ruger's division out from town intending to force a way through and continue the retreat on the main road. To his pleasant surprise, no evidence of the Rebels was found at Thompson's Station beyond smoldering campfires, and the Federals took possession of the crossroads without opposition.

Schofield ordered his headquarters troop, under chief engineer Captain William J. Twining, to go at full gallop down the road toward Franklin and telegraph the situation to Nashville. Twining was also instructed to examine the means of crossing the river. Schofield then sat on his horse and listened until he could no longer hear the clatter of hoofs on the hard road in the distance, satisfied that the road to Franklin was indeed clear.

Turning and riding back to Spring Hill, Schofield found that General Cox had just come in with his division, representing the rear of the army. Ordering Cox to take the advance at once and march to Franklin, Schofield instructed Stanley to take charge of the trains once more and follow immediately behind Cox. It was sometime past midnight, and the march continued all through the night, the head of Cox's column approaching the outskirts of Franklin about four-thirty on the morning of November 30.

A "run of luck" had gone in favor of the Union. Clearly Schofield had risked much in staying so long at Columbia. The chances of placing his army in a difficult position were too great when compared with gaining a little more time for Thomas to concentrate troops at Nashville. Just as Hood underestimated what Schofield could do, Schofield seems to have underestimated what Hood could do. While the Confederates might not have been able to take the town, the pike was another story. At any time for several hours before midnight, at the least, they might have captured and held the pike in force either north or south of Spring Hill. The result would not necessarily have been disastrous for Schofield, but that it would have presented problems is undeniable.

Hood was enraged to learn at daylight that he had underrated what Schofield could accomplish, discovering that the Union commander had eluded him while he slept. "Wrathy as a rattlesnake" was the phrase General Brown applied in describing Hood's

The Nathaniel Cheairs House, where Hood and several of his generals
ate breakfast and quarreled on the morning of November 30, 1864.
[*Photograph by Rudy E. Sanders.*]

demeanor. Many of the Confederate generals ate breakfast at the home of Major Nat Cheairs, and several tempers were short. Stories have come down in local tradition of a near violent quarrel. In the midst of angry accusations of neglect, demands for apology, and a generally tense atmosphere, Hood furiously lashed out at his subordinates, placing the blame on them rather than on himself.

"The best move in my career as a soldier," he wrote later in his memoirs, "I was thus destined to behold come to naught." Primarily he blamed Cheatham. Always a controversial figure— Braxton Bragg had earlier attempted to shift blame for his own problems at Stones River to Cheatham, accusing him of being intoxicated—Cheatham would be accused by Hood of errors at Spring Hill leading to failure, although a military court later cleared Cheatham of all charges. According to Hood's story, he rode up to Cheatham at twilight on November 29 and exlaimed, "General, why in the name of God have you not attacked the enemy and taken possession of that pike?" Pungently, Cheatham later stated in reply that any such dramatic scene "only occurred in the imagination of General Hood." The bitter polemics of Hood and Cheatham serve little beyond demonstrating that, as the British military historian Sir Basil H. Liddell-Hart observed in his biography of Sherman, "amid the uncertainties of war mistakes must be made," but "nobody knows the general who admits that he has made one."

Clearly Hood had made mistakes, and, as the army's commander, his was the main responsibility for failure. The breakdown of command responsibility and communication was appalling. The general's planning was vague. He did not remain on the field to see that his orders were carried out. He seemed lacking in energy and aggressiveness. Finally, he was overconfident.

Cheatham was also deserving of blame. Repeatedly during the late afternoon, whether due to a misunderstanding of Hood's intention or to some other reason, he contradicted Hood's order to seize the pike, changing direction to the north and attempting to take Spring Hill, only to at last break off all activity, without authority, about or shortly after 6 P.M. He seems to have made little or no effort to keep Hood informed of what was transpiring either in the late afternoon or during the night. Strange also was his inertia relative to possible enemy movements on the pike. Even before receiving Hood's order to fire at any one marching on the pike, which came sometime after midnight, Cheatham had already been warned by one of his staff that troops were moving on the road. Never did he personally investigate the pike; he was content to let the matter rest after receiving Johnson's report that all was quiet.

Curiously, too, General Stewart had shown little interest in blocking the road, although his men were relatively fresh. As to Forrest, Captain H. A. Tyler claimed that he and the general sat on their horses near Spring Hill about dark, helplessly watching the Federals passing, until finally Forrest threw up a clenched fist and said: "————Hood! Had he supported me here as he promised, that whole army would have been our prisoners." Perhaps so, but even the normally aggressive cavalry leader did hardly anything to block the pike north of Spring Hill. Jackson's division held it only a few minutes before retiring, and Forrest reported nothing to Hood. Maybe, of course, he thought it useless.

Even had Hood placed his entire command astride the Columbia–Franklin Pike, Schofield would still have held alternate routes to Franklin and Nashville. He could have used the railroad bed that passed west of Spring Hill. Farther west, the Carter's Creek Pike presented a good road to Franklin. Even farther to the west, Schofield could have skirted Franklin, marching by a country road to the old pike to Nashville from Hillsboro. While he may not have been aware of the last, he certainly knew of the first two possibilities.

Nor was Schofield's position at Spring Hill weak. Hood did not have the vastly superior numbers with which some have credited him. By seven o'clock in the evening, when Stewart was wandering lost on a country road east of the village, Schofield had two divisions and his artillery at Spring Hill. Two more divisions were only a few miles to the south, nearing the outskirts of the town. Shortly after midnight, all the Union force had either reached Spring Hill or passed on toward Franklin.

And possibly the day was simply too short. One of the most difficult matters to calculate is whether the Rebels, even if Hood and his subordinates knew precisely what they were about and had made no mistakes, had sufficient time on a short November day to march 20,000 men on miserable country roads from Duck River to Spring Hill and deploy them for effective action against entrenched Federal troops. At least fifteen miles had to be traversed from Davis' Ford, where Hood crossed his infantry, to Spring Hill. And some of the soldiers had to march two to five miles before they even reached the ford.

Neither army commander is particularly impressive in this episode, but realizing that the head of Hood's infantry column was still two and a half miles from Spring Hill at three o'clock; that the Federals had 6,500 or 7,000 men entrenched at the village as early as two o'clock (supported by artillery while Confederate artillery was at Columbia); that the first Rebel infantry did not get into position to render assistance to Forrest's cavalry, which was virtually out of ammunition, until about four o'clock; and that sunset came at four thirty, with darkness following in forty minutes, it seems reasonable to conclude that the Confederate chances to destroy Schofield's force have been magnified in some accounts.

This is certainly not to say that the Rebel flanking movement was utterly hopeless. The contest for Spring Hill was so close—if Forrest had been only a bit earlier, at noon for instance—that a slight change might have made all the difference in the ultimate result. A more capable Confederate commander, even a more healthy Hood, might have been able to eliminate some of the delay and confusion in organizing Confederate ranks for an assault in time to drive Stanley from Spring Hill before Schofield could reinforce him.

But once it became clear that Confederate efforts to drive Stanley out of Spring Hill were not going to succeed, Hood's alternatives were limited. If he had succeeded in taking the pike south of the village, his troops would have been placed between the two portions of the Union army, possibly in a more dangerous position than that of their enemy. The best move for Hood was to make a lodgement on the pike north of Spring Hill. This was what Schofield feared most. But even taking the pike on the north would not have eliminatred the possibility of the Yankees moving to the west and continuing the retreat.

In any event, Schofield did not have to continue his withdrawl. Stanley was well positioned defensively at Spring Hill. The Federals had all their trains and artillery and almost as many soldiers—maybe *as* many—as Hood could marshall. Schofield might have placed the rest of his army in position and accepted battle at Spring Hill with a very good chance of successfully throwing back a Rebel attack.

Schofield had escaped, but the strange inertia of key Confederate officers remains a puzzle. Attempts to unravel what happened and why never quite seem to explain. The suspicion of something more lingers. Were the rumors of wild parties merely spice to the Spring Hill legend? Or might there have been some germ of truth therein?

Captain H. A. Tyler of Forrest's command, who was quoted earlier, also told of seeing a woman standing on the front porch of a house at Spring Hill, "just as the sun was setting." Tyler said he rode up and "stopped at the gate, when she came out and joined me. I was struck by her great beauty, and began at once asking her about the roads and the lay of the ground. After giving me the information, she asked what troops those were. I told her Buford's Division of Forrest's Cavalry. She at once asked if General Forrest was with us, and I pointed him out to her. She then said she would like to meet him and speak to him. I said, 'Who are you, madam?' and she replied: 'Mrs. Peters. General Forrest will know me.' I, of course, knew her too," said Tyler, who immediately galloped back and "told General Forrest that Mrs. Peters wished to see him. I took him to her and left them talking. . . ."

Some persons might be inclined to "read between the lines" of such an account as Tyler's; on the other hand, the situation could certainly have been completely innocent. Colonel Henry Stone, assistant adjutant general on Thomas's staff, explained the Spring Hill failure of the Confederates a few years later, stating that "there were queer doings in the rebel lines among some of the leading officers. Nearly two years before," Stone explained, "the rebel General Van Dorn had been shot to death by the infuriated husband of a fascinating woman who lived in a large mansion near Spring Hill. As the rebel army now approached, he left for Nashville, but she remained behind. There was music and dancing and feasting, and other gods than Mars were worshipped. During the sacrificing at their shrines," concluded Stone, "the whole of Schofield's . . . force moved silently and fearfully by. . . . But in the morning there was much swearing. . . . Cheatham and Forrest and the others who had given themselves up to the charms of society the night before were more chagrined at the disappearance of the enemy than at their own lapse from duty."

Fact or legend? One wonders. Perhaps the greatest significance of the fiasco at Spring Hill was its effect on General Hood's behavior. Even worse than placing responsibility on his corps and division commanders for the failure to gain the pike and block the Federals, the Rebel commander unfairly blamed the soldiers in his army. "Grave concern," Hood wrote, troubled him upon "the discovery that the Army, after a forward march of 180 miles, was still seemingly unwilling to accept battle unless under the protection of breastworks." The general continued in a vein that reveals more about his own state of mind than that of the army, especially his unwillingness to accept responsibility for his own shortcomings. "In my inmost heart," he said, "I questioned whether or not I would ever succeed in eradicating this evil." There is no evidence, other than Hood's biased interpretation, that the affair at Spring Hill was due to any faltering of the Confederate soldiers. Confusion there was, certainly; but not any lack of Rebel courage.

Now, however, all of Hood's months of frustration welled up within. Tired and distraught—perhaps *sick* is not too strong a term—he was too emotionally unhinged to command. Worst of all possible conclusions, the general somehow imagined that for purposes of discipline and restoration of élan what the army needed was to make a frontal assault.

# 4 /

# *They Were the Very Last*

Onward through the morning Hood rode in the vanguard of Stewart's infantry corps in an attempt to catch up with Schofield. The Nashville pike wound across hills and through bluegrass bottoms. The road and ditches were littered with the debris of Schofield's night march. Dead horses and mules lay in the road, cut from their traces. Burned wagons had been pushed to the roadside by frantic teamsters. Forrest's cavalry was somewhere ahead of the infantry column, harassing Schofield's weary rear guard on the trek to Franklin.

By noon, Hood and Stewart's advance had arrived in a small valley some three and one-half miles south of Franklin, on the south side of the Winstead-Breezy Hill range. The high ridges formed the southern border of the plain of Franklin. Now the regimental flags of Wagner's division, which formed Schofield's rear guard, dotted the cedar-lined slopes.

The chronology of events among the Confederate high command for the next few hours is difficult to ascertain because of conflicting reports. Some things, however, can be grasped from tangled threads of evidence. Evidently Hood's first mission was to drive Wagner's division from the range of hills. Consequently, Stewart was ordered to veer eastward from the Columbia Pike onto the present-day Henpeck Lane, which would lead him one and one-half miles to the Lewisburg pike. The Lewisburg road paralleled the Nashville pike into Franklin. Stewart's mission was to march his advance as far as the Lewisburg road and then turn the entire column northward through the fields and hills to force Wagner from the ridge.

Meanwhile Hood rested at his first battle headquarters in the Harrison house. The imposing brick structure stands today on the west side of the Nashville road, in the valley south of Winstead Hill. Somehow the Harrison place became associated totally with the tragedy of the war's carnage. Only two months before Hood's arrival, the cavalryman General John H. Kelly had been brought here to die, wounded in a hard fight nearby. And that very night of November 30, one of Hood's brigade leaders, General John C. Carter, would be taken here mortally wounded. Here as well, the sullen, angry Hood planned his strategy which would send over 1,500 men to their deaths on the Franklin plain.

Even before Wagner's division abandoned the heights that blocked Hood's view of the town, the Confederate officer obviously was determined to attack at Franklin. Stewart's orders for the flanking march via Henpeck Lane made this clear. Stewart reported later that his movement was carried out for such a purpose. "In compliance with the instructions of the commanding general I moved to the right toward the Harpeth River and formed to attack the enemy. . . . Cheatham's corps was also formed to attack, and the two corps were to move forward simultaneously."

Hood's first view of the Federal entrenchments surrounding the village of Franklin came shortly after 1 P.M. Stewart's flanking march had forced Wagner to withdraw. With his crutch strapped to the saddle, Hood rode up the eminence to see the Franklin plain.

Already Forrest had arrived and was the first officer to counsel against a direct assault on Schofield's position. The level ground, with few groves of trees or hill obstructions on the terrain due north, could not hide the strength of the Union position. The breastworks astride the Nashville road were visible enough. So were the Yankee artillery positions north and east of the Harpeth River, which could subject any attacking column to an enfilade fire. Forrest did not require a spyglass to realize the peril. His campaign of 1863 in Franklin had made him aware of the strength of the position.

Forrest knew as well that Schofield was vulnerable on the extreme eastern flank of the Union line. Upstream from Franklin, there were fords available for crossing. Forrest begged Hood for the use of his own troopers and a single infantry division. He promised Hood that he would force Schofield from his works on the south bank.

The William Harrison House, where two Confederate generals, John H. Kelly and John C. Carter, died of their wounds. Also, Hood and Forrest here disagreed about the plans for an assault at Franklin.

[*Photograph by Rudy E. Sanders.*]

Hood refused and, as Cheatham's advance appeared on the road, began to fashion a precise mode of attack. Somehow, by 3 P.M., he had committed his army to a suicidal assault. Behind on the road from Columbia, General Stephen Lee's corps and practically all of Hood's artillery were still on the march. Hood would assail the Franklin works with only some 18,000 infantry of the corps led by Frank Cheatham and A.P. Stewart. Artillery support would be virtually non-existent. Stewart, for example, had only a single battery on the field and would be forced to disperse it among three infantry divisions.

Why did Hood attack? It was not the product of bad advice. Already in the first hours at the Harrison house, Hood had announced this intention in a council of war. Various generals had protested that such a move would produce a senseless loss of life. Then came the urgings of Forrest for a flanking maneuver. Later, other generals, such as Frank Cheatham and Pat Cleburne, attempted to dissuade Hood from giving such an order.

Hood would not be moved. He stood on his crutches under a tree in the early afternoon, on the approximate site of the present-day battlefield map astride Winstead Hill. Finally the Kentuckian returned the field glasses to a leather case, turned, and announced, "We will make the fight!"

Dreams die hard, and Hood later attempted to explain the decision that sent his army to its doom. Sometimes the explanations were contradictory. Later, in February 1865, a broken, defeated officer attempted in his official report to explain his motives for the assault. The primary reason here was that Hood, through captured intelligence, knew of General George Thomas's strong position at Nashville and of how the Federals intended to hold and strengthen the Franklin position. So Schofield must be assailed before such strengthening could be accomplished, or before Schofield "should escape at Franklin" and "gain the works" around Nashville. Even these reasons in a single report were contradictory and do not mesh well with other explanations. Years later, when Hood at New Orleans penned his angry reminiscence, *Advance and Retreat*, there was no mention of any thought that Schofield intended to stay and strengthen the Franklin position; now the reason was solely the desire to crush the Federals before they retreated into the haven of the impregnable fortifications at Nashville. And on the afternoon of the battle, Hood sent word to the brigade commanders of Cleburne's division explaining not only the method of assault but also why it was necessary. At this point, Hood's reasoning was that if the Confederates took Franklin, Nashville would fall—a city he described as the key to the independence of the Southern Confederacy.

Probably this last explanation, recalled in 1907 by General D.C. Govan, came closest to the truth. It reflected the irrational dreams and visions that possessed Hood on the pike between Columbia and the Franklin field. Certainly the post-battle explanations not only contradict each other but give as well evidence of hasty and poor reasoning. If Hood intended to crush Schofield before he improved the Franklin position, why could he not have waited a few scant hours for the arrival of the remainder of his infantry and his artillery? Moreover, the comments regarding the urgency of crushing Schofield prior to some union with a strong Federal position at Nashville do not jibe with what Hood apparently knew on the long march from the Tennessee River to the Nashville basin. As mentioned earlier, the evidence is strong that Hood never grasped the reality that General George Thomas was assembling a powerful army at Nashville which could have overwhelmed him even without Schofield's presence. Indeed, there is little evidence that Hood ever understood that any serious impediment to his ambitions was present in Middle Tennessee except Schofield's awaiting infantry down the slopes in the Franklin valley.

Somehow all of the elements of John Bell Hood's personality had come together on the cedar-lined hillside on the afternoon of November 30. Of course he was the product of his own Southern time and place. Maybe the Franklin carnage went back to Dr. John W. Hood's large farm on Somerset Creek in Clark County, Kentucky, to a world of slaves, worship of power, adulation of weaponry and horsemanship. The young six-foot, two-inch Hood, with his broad shoulders and blond-auburn hair, had been reared in a dream world of chivalric power. He had been the young, handsome epitome of Southern excess—too much gambling, drinking, and horse racing. It had been easy and natural. Physician Hood's farm with its slave cabins had represented the best of a culture that placed a premium on physical assertion.

Subsequent years at West Point and army life on the Great Plains gave evidence of other things. Hood was always reckless. The *Orders U.S. Corps of Cadets* recounted Hood's miserable conduct record at the military academy. By the end of his senior year, Hood had acquired 196 demerits and stood on the verge of expulsion from West Point. It was the pattern of his life. Reckless conduct had caused him to lose a quarter of his command in the Comanche attack on Devil's River in 1856. Carelessness had produced the chidings by Robert E. Lee on the Virginia front, when inspections of Hood's camps showed evidence of neglect.

Neglect of detail had haunted the long march from Palmetto to Franklin. There had never been a real plan. Hood's aims had changed repeatedly, at Kennesaw, Cedartown, La Fayettte, Gadsden, near Guntersville, and elsewhere. Neglect had produced the long delay at Tuscumbia and Florence until the approach of Forrest's cavalry and the arrival of supplies. The march from Florence to Columbia was ill-planned to entrap Schofield, if that was its intention. The flanking march from Columbia to Spring Hill was a textbook demonstration of poor command supervision.

The same careless—even reckless—behavior was now evident on the Winstead–Breezy Hill range. Hood could have awaited the arrival of General Stephen Lee's corps, which would have added another precious 8,000 infantry to the assault column. Perhaps the army's field guns could have reduced some of the advantage Schofield enjoyed in the strong earthworks. Later, in his memoirs, Hood maintained that he deliberately avoided using artillery at Franklin because it would have posed a threat to women and children in the village. This is sheer fantasy. Hood *did* use what artillery was available in the assault. Two batteries were on the field and one was assigned to each corps.

Perhaps Hood's reason for ordering the army forward that afternoon involved something deep in his soul. Perhaps the attack orders came because John Bell Hood was at once what he had been always and what he had become in the last year.

In part, the suicidal attack was characteristic of what the Kentuckin had been for most of his life. Always Hood had been one to act rather than think. Hood by nature was a gambler. There were army tales of how he once put a thousand dollars on one card in a faro game and emerged victorious. Gambling evidently had been one of his early sins in the days on the Kentucky farm. Somehow, in the years between boyhood and a division command in Robert E. Lee's Army of Northern Virginia, Hood had fashioned for himself a self-image—aided by the responses of admirers—as the ultimate Southern extremist, the self-stylized cavalier who raged larger than life.

And this image had served him well during earlier days in the Civil War. Well might Lee chide his young lieutenant for careless management of his army camps. But certainly Lee admired Hood's boldness. After all, within three years, Hood was elevated from an obscure second lieutenant to the prestigious level of lieutenant-general.

Hood's meteoric rise to acclaim had come with the shedding of much blood. Somehow others had paid always for his boldness, as did troopers of the Second Cavalry that day in Texas on the Devil's River. It was a pattern that by the advent of the Civil war was well established. In battle and in the drawing room, Hood demonstrated his aggressive nature while serving in Lee's army. In battle, his commands were consistent in boasting high rates of killed and wounded. At Second Manassas, Hood's Texas brigade lost 42 percent of its strength. At Sharpsburg, the division led by Hood was virtually wiped out; only 318 men survived in the hapless Texas brigade. Hood never abandoned his headlong tactics of attack. After all, his idols, Lee and "Stonewall" Jackson, were masters of the infantry assault. And, frankly, Hood's aggressive reputation had won him extremely rapid promotion.

His advance was a case of too much and too soon. Hood was changing by the autumn of 1863. Perhaps the newly displayed burning ambition developed because Hood felt he had something to prove, with his lost leg, useless arm, and new fiancée. Clearly Hood became a sycophant who fawned upon every word of President Jefferson Davis and told that beleaguered leader what he wished to hear. Hood's attentions were rewarded; soon he led a corps in the Army of Tennessee.

The dishonest flavor of Hood's secret correspondence to Richmond from northern Virginia displayed his ambition, but it also revealed something else. Hood wanted to be a Robert E. Lee but lacked three vital things possessed by the Virginian. Hood's lack of character was revealed by the obvious dishonesty of his secret letters, and again by the way in which he continually blamed his officers and men for failure. Lee would have done neither.

Second, Hood, once in command of the Army of Tennessee, attempted to direct the army in the fashion used by Lee in Virginia. From Atlanta to Spring Hill, Hood had come to grief by the loose nature of his overall command system. Lee had actually directed his corps leaders, "Stonewall" Jackson and James Longstreet, in a rather informal fashion. General plans were drawn up, but the details were left to the corps officers, and, in some instances, they were allowed broad discretion to alter details. But men such as Stewart, Cheatham, and others—although good officers—were no Jacksons or Longstreets. Moreover, Jackson and Longstreet could operate with knowledge that their commanding general would support them even in failure and shoulder the responsibility for failure. With Hood's generals, it was different. How could they trust him enough to take responsibility on their own? They could well remember the fate of General William Hardee in the Atlanta campaign.

Finally, Hood came to the slopes of Winstead and Breezy hills with what he considered to be the tactics Lee would use. Attack was all that Hood knew. It was, again, the pattern of a life, molded into his personality years before the Civil War. Lee's use of the tactical offensive had only reinforced something already present in the Kentuckian's nature. Maybe other things reinforced it as well—frustration over the failures at Atlanta, the burning desire to prove something to Sally ("Buck") Preston in Richmond, physical and mental pain over his frightful wounds, and other matters. Perhaps it was a display of temper over the fiasco at Spring Hill. Some might suggest that Hood's decision came because he was a Southerner. Grady McWhiney and Perry Jamieson, in *Attack and Die: Civil War Military Tactics and the Southern Heritage*, even traced the martial spirit of Hood and his comrades to the same Celtic love of attack that had characterized battles long past such as Telamon, Bannockburn, and Culloden.

Perhaps all or at least some of these reasons were there on the Indian Summer day. One was there for certain. Hood wanted to be a Lee. The irony is that Hood did not realize that the war had changed even Lee's mode of combat. The war on the eastern front had passed Hood by since the campaign at Gettysburg. The long miles of trenches at Richmond and Petersburg were more akin to the First World War than to the derring-do open-field assaults Hood could remember from the Seven Days or Gettysburg. Besides, Lee—like Hood now—was too weak in men and artillery to fight in the old style.

But Hood had not changed. All of these old things drove

him on now. He was driven as well, perhaps, by that mythical Confederate dream of sweeping to the Ohio River, reclaiming Tennessee and Kentucky, and planting the flag on midwestern flatlands. More than once it had stirred the Confederate soul, as it had done in 1862, when Generals Braxton Bragg and Edmund Kirby Smith moved northward into Kentucky.

So in the early afternoon of November 30, 1864, Hood closed the case that held his field glasses and announced that the attack would come. It was the act of a tormented man driven by visions and dreams.

Hood was not the only person whose soul was fired with zeal on the slopes of Winstead Hill. By 3 P.M. the veterans of Cheatham's corps, many of them Tennesseans, had come up the pike from Columbia. As Cheatham's men moved onto the slopes of Winstead and Breezy hills, the Tennessee troops reportedly broke into loud cheers when they gazed down into the bluegrass plain at Franklin. They were coming home!

Young Captain Theodrick Carter probably cheered as well. Down the pike a few miles distant was a brick farmhouse standing hard by the Nashville pike. If young Tod Carter possessed a pair of field glasses, probably he searched for a glimpse of his home place. Perhaps he wondered if his father, Fountain Branch Carter, and other family members were there today. The saga of Tod Carter and his brothers was in truth the story of the Army of Tennessee.

Tod Carter and his two brothers, Moscow and Francis, had joined the army on the same day in May 1861. All had been in Company H, Twentieth Tennessee Infantry. Such units were the object of much community pride. Before being marched off to camps of instruction, companies of Middle Tennessee boys were treated to stump oratory by local politicians, fried chicken feasts, the accolades of young women, and other such honors. Typical was the saga of Company E, Third Tennessee Infantry, which had been organized the same month in nearby Spring Hill. As usual, a prominent local citizen—in this case Nat Cheairs—was chosen as captain. Spring Hill women made uniforms and tents. There was a ceremony where the ladies of the community presented the unit— dubbed the Brown Rifles—with a flag and sword. A farewell sermon was delivered at the Methodist Church, a local band sere-

Captain Theodrick (Tod) Carter.

naded, and then the excited young men were off to the Great Adventure.

Tod Carter, his brothers, and the other Middle Tennessee boys soon had their hopes dashed. The war became boredom in dirty army encampments, with poor and scant food or dysentery. It became the carnage of battle where the casualty lists from Murfreesboro or Chickamauga could produce overwhelming grief in a single country village. The Carter family's saga in the war was typical of that of their neighbors. Moscow Carter, later elected a lieutenant colonel, had been captured early in 1862; now he was down the slope at the Carter home, serving out his parole. Eighteen-year-old Francis Carter's hopes for glory were dashed when he was wounded severely at the battle of Shiloh, spent months in a hospital, and was discharged from the army in late 1862.

Tod Carter was the last, and the men around him also were the last, ghostly remnants of what had once been the mighty Army of Tennessee. Once it had been a fearsome agent of destruction that had almost demolished Grant's reputation at Shiloh. It had struck terror into the hearts of the midwestern folk in 1862 when the long gray line and miles of wagons moved forward toward the Ohio River. At Chickamauga it had cut General William Rosecrans's army in two, sending a panicked General and half of his army in flight to Chattanooga. Like a defiant wounded animal, the army had awaited Sherman in North Georgia.

Sherman came, and still the Army of Tennessee was a powerful force. In the long campaign from Dalton through New Hope Church to Atlanta and Jonesboro, the Army of Tennessee was bled at an awful cost it could never repay. Even after the May campaign and the fighting from Dalton to New Hope Church, General Joseph Johnston had listed over 82,000 soldiers "aggregate present," now Hood's listing of men "aggregate present" did not reach 45,000. Worse, Hood on the Franklin slopes had scarcely 25,688 infantry listed as "effective."

Tod Carter and his comrades were part of the last. Perhaps the field return for General George Thomas's forces in Tennessee and Kentucky on November 20 told the story. The Civil War had become by 1864 a coldly analytical process of men and machines. Even without the services of General A.J. Smith's divisions from St. Louis, scheduled for arrival within days, Thomas and Schofield together on that day could field against Hood over 100,000 men listed as "aggregate present" and a solid 81,845 described as "present for duty."

The story was told as well in the sounds of factory and locomotive whistles. Back in Palmetto, Georgia, Hood and his staff had estimated that 600 supply wagons would be needed for a forward move into Tennessee. Only 300 were to be had, many pulled by weary, ill-fed animals. Meanwhile, in the debacle of the loss of Atlanta and Georgia itself, Hood's ragged army had lost its entire reserve supply of ammunition, tons of war material, and hundreds of thousands of food rations. So decrepit were the commissary and quartermaster resources that Hood's entire forward movement was stalled at Florence, Alabama, until the Memphis and Charleston Railroad, some of its track overgrown with weeds, could be repaired and meager foodstuffs obtained.

The well-fed bluecoats who awaited Hood's attack on the Franklin plain suffered from no such problems. The Industrial Revolution had enlisted on the Union side in the Civil War, and by 1864 technology was as vital as several infantry corps on a battlefield. Sherman's advance into Georgia had already proved this earlier in the year.

The push of the Yankees on the western front into the Confederate Heartland had been as much a victory for technology as for infantry within the breastworks. The story of Sherman's rail network serves only as a single example of how the war had changed. When Sherman invaded Georgia, there was bold talk among Confederate leaders of how they could disrupt the rail line of supply and communication that extended north and west via Chattanooga and Nashville to Louisville. But in January 1864, Sherman had appointed Colonel W.E. Merrill as chief engineer of the Army of the Cumberland. Merrill, a man with an engineer's way of thinking, had designed scores of stout log and iron blockhouses—replete with ventilators and independent water resources—to withstand any lightning Rebel cavalry raid.

Once the rail line was secure, Sherman turned to the overwhelming industrial resources of the North. The numbers of locomotives and rolling stock that moved through northern Georgia were almost incredible. Boxcars bore names such as "Delaware and Lackawanna," while locomotives were brought from midwestern towns. Whole regiments of engineers were assembled for standby duty in case a rail line was broken. Huge shops at

Chattanooga would furnish any needed parts. Other engineer units were made available for the almost instant rebuilding of bridges. For example, on May 15, the Army of Tennessee had destroyed the large span across the Oostanaula River when it abandoned the position at Resaca. Within five days Sherman's trains were crossing the river. The war had changed.

How much did they understand of this, the very last of a great army, as they stood that afternoon on the Franklin slopes? Surely something had brought them there, and surely something as well would explain why they would attack that afternoon with such fierceness. Surely it was not devotion to John Bell Hood. Always rumors within the Army of Tennessee had circulated with ease. The men could not have been unaware that Hood had repeatedly accused them of virtual cowardice. Earlier, in August and September, Hood repeatedly had rebuked them for what he considered a lack of valor. Even in this modern era, there is a chill that comes when one reads Hood's complaints to the government after his failure in the Atlanta campaign. Shortly after the abandonment of Atlanta, he had informed Richmond that "there is a tacit if not expressed determination among the men of this army, extending to officers as high in some instances as colonel, that they will not attack breastworks."

The men did not read that dispatch. Nor did they read a note Hood sent to Richmond in early November explaining away the defeat at Jonesboro as the act of cowardice on the part of his troops. To prove "what a disgraceful effort was made by our men," Hood included the casualty rates of killed and wounded.

They had not read these letters, but they knew Hood. Their diaries or letters penned in the dusty Georgia camps of 1864 or on the long march into Tennessee contain no expressions of love and admiration for Hood as one could find in the case of earlier leaders such as Albert Sidney Johnston or Beauregard. No one patted the mane of Hood's horse, but soldiers had touched the bald head of General Joseph Johnston and called him "Old Joe."

They had not come to Winstead Hill for Hood. But something had brought them there. There was an electric sentiment in the air, almost a sullen determination to prove that Hood's disparagements were untrue. Certainly Hood was not the only man on the slope who had felt frustration and humiliation because Schofield had eluded the grand trap at Spring Hill. The Army of Tennessee

72  ]

had a long, sad record of command discord. In the spring of 1863 camps had echoed with the talk of strife between Braxton Bragg and his generals as to the lack of success in the Kentucky invasion and the hard fight at Murfreesboro. These men were absolute veterans, the hard core, and knew as well of the uprising against Bragg after Chickamauga, a near-mutiny that compelled President Jefferson Davis himself to come to Georgia as a peacemaker. Occasionally their later letters and diaries were sprinkled with knowledge of other quarrels—Bragg and Longstreet at Chattanooga . . . the long, bitter disputes between Jefferson Davis and Joseph Johnston . . . the impasse after the Atlanta battles that lost to the army the services of Hardee and others.

But the record does indicate that on that Indian summer afternoon, the men of Cheatham's and Stewart's commands came to the ridge with a special anger and frustration. Certainly General Pat Cleburne had these feelings on the route from Spring Hill. After the stormy breakfast at the Cheairs' house, Cleburne had ridden to Winstead Hill with his Arkansas comrade, General D.C. Govan, who recalled that he had never seen the Irishman so despondent. Cleburne felt that Hood had blamed him for the Spring Hill fiasco. En route he called aside another friend, General John C. Brown. Brown waited until his column had passed and then talked with his fellow division leader. Cleburne was "deeply hurt" and felt that Hood was blaming him for the previous night's episode. Cleburne, one of the Confederacy's finest division leaders, was mortified by the implications that he had mismanaged his command. The conversation with Brown was terminated when orders arrived from headquarters. "We will resume this conversation at the first convenient moment," Cleburne muttered as he rode away.

Only hours later, Cleburne would fall beneath the Yankee breastworks in an attack he knew was suicidal. A last conversation with General D.C. Govan told much about Cleburne's own hopes for success. Already he had requested of Hood that he be allowed to advance the division in columns instead of lines—an alignment that would subject the rebel infantry to far less punishment. Later, in his memoir, Hood attempted to justify his attack plan by recounting an alleged conversation with Cleburne on the hill. According to Hood, Cleburne insisted that he had more faith then in the final outcome of the Confederate effort than he had felt at any previous time in the war. Hood's record for veracity already had been tested

and found wanting in the dismal intrigue prior to the battles of Atlanta. His description of Cleburne's disposition on the ridge that afternoon is probably absolute fantasy. Cleburne was angry and discouraged. He intended to ask for an investigation of the Spring Hill affair after the present campaign had been completed. Close associates recalled his despondent attitude. Perhaps the Irishman's mood was summed up best in one of his last conversations with his brigade leader, Govan. Govan recalled that Cleburne and the other officers realized the desperate nature of what Hood intended to do. The columns were forming as Govan prepared to ride back to his own command. He paused and observed that few of the men would ever return to Arkansas after the battle. Cleburne replied that if they were to die, they should die like men.

★ ★ ★

MANY would perish on that November afternoon and even into the dark night hours when one could scarcely distinguish the rifle fire of enemy and friend. Why would they march down the slope in the late afternoon, moving against breastworks that from the hill even without field glasses would appear impregnable?

Dreams die hard, and the visions of something had not yet vanished when the ghostly remnants of what once had been a mighty army appeared on Winstead Hill. Certainly there was that day a general frustration with the sorry events that had occurred at Spring Hill. But that episode does not explain the fierce determination that the men of Cheatham's and Stewart's commands would display. After all, these infantry were the last of what once had been a mighty column.

For three years the Army of Tennessee had been wracked with command disputes, and the rumors of what had transpired at Spring Hill to most of them were only another incident in a long saga of misadventures. They did not march against the Franklin trenches only because they were frustrated by Spring Hill's debacle. Perhaps that explained in part their conduct, but that was not all of the matter. These men were veterans and victims of command dispute, because the western army had never made peace with itself.

How many times they had stood on some symbolic ridge

General Patrick R. Cleburne.

like the slopes of Winstead and Breezy hills! Some could remember the command turmoil in icy February 1862 at Fort Donelson. What followed was no different. There was the confusion between Beauregard and Albert Sidney Johnston as to the plans for Shiloh . . . Beauregard's subsequent quarrel with Richmond . . . the incredible mismanagement of the Kentucky invasion by Bragg and Edmund Kirby Smith . . . the post-Murfreesboro strife between Bragg and his officers, and many other entanglements.

Even if the previous night's frustration was a factor, the men of the Army of Tennessee advanced that afternoon for two other reasons. One was because they were Southerners, fighting for some intangible reason. They were no army of planters' sons, nor was their companion Army of Northern Virginia. Some were sons of slaveowners and others were children of yeoman farmers who owned no blacks, or were of shopkeepers in some Southern village. They had come together in 1861 from hundreds of Southern towns and hamlets, from Lynchburg, Tennessee, to Eufala, Alabama. Southerners defy and fear analysis, and in the long run they would have spurned the process of explanation.

The saga of the Army of Tennessee is preserved in the letters and diaries of the men. They are locked away in the vaults of the Tennessee State Archives, the library at Tulane Univesity, the archives of Alabama, the Library of Congress, Huntington Library in California, and a score of other repositories. These documents all contain vague statements about the Southern "cause."

Exactly what that cause was is difficult to ascertain. Something had moved Tod Carter's friends to organize Company H of the Twentieth Tennessee. Perhaps it was a vague dream, obscure in part because they were Southern boys who spurned the quality of analysis. They were part of a Southern Confederacy whose leaders had never analyzed exactly what were the war's aims and how one meshed aims with military policy. Dixie never possessed a genuine commanding general until the appointment of General Robert E. Lee in the last month or so of the conflict. Even the correspondence of Lee, Jefferson Davis, and other Confederate chieftains contains little on the precise nature of the rebellion, save for some obscure statements regarding "independence." What was the South trying to do? In the eyes of the men of Cheatham and Stewart that afternoon, what was the nature of the fight? Was it something designed to create a separate nation beset with a continuing slaveocracy? Was the dream to be a new land south of the Ohio and Potomac eventually to be free from the system of black chattels? Or was the South destined to return to the old Union under its own terms? Was the attack something to be carried out because they were Southern? Did that not mean scorn for Northerners, however obscure the image, or even a near self-destructive resolve to strive even if failure seemed imminent?

Probably it involved all of that, but in the case of young Tod Carter and his comrades there was something else. Their comrades in the Army of Northern Virginia shared all of these resolves and questions. But the weary infantry on the ridge that afternoon was driven by something very special—that great dream to gain the Ohio River for the Confederacy. Back in the early days, not long after companies had been organized in Franklin and Spring Hill, something had been taken away from them. Nashville had been considered the great bastion of the western Confederacy. Prior to the Civil War, it had been the most cosmopolitan city south of the Ohio River except for New Orleans. In 1860, Nashville had boasted five daily newspapers, gas lights, an active theater, the medical school at the University of Nashville, and other evidences of progress and sophistication. The city's daily affairs, in part, were controlled by the planter-merchant class whom writer Alfred Leland Crabb decades later described as the "Nashville Gods." They were men of substance and power, who resided mainly in the hills and bluegrass fields south of the city, in residences such as Belle Meade, Traveler's Rest, Belmont, or Glen Leven.

At first the advent of war had done little to sully the image. After all, Nashville in 1861 was the great manufacturing center of the western Confederacy. Foundries wrought artillery, made percussion caps for rifles, or fashioned saddles and blankets. Nearby, on the Cumberland River, powder mills were the main source of Confederate gunpowder when the war began. West of Nashville, in the stubborn hill country between the Tennessee and Cumberland rivers, stretching from the Kentucky border to Alabama, lay the Great Western Iron Belt. In 1861 it was the South's main source for pig, wrought, and bar iron needed for artillery and other uses.

Nashville in 1861 had been the great western citadel of the Confederacy, but the walls had crumbled soon. The surrender of Fort Donelson in February 1862 had led to the Confederate abandonment of the city amid chaos. Mobs surged into warehouses to seize precious stores of bacon and other foodstuffs. Meanwhile the remaining remnants of the original army of the western front had straggled southward into Alabama to regroup prior to Shiloh and to strive to retake the Mother Earth of the Tennessee and Kentucky bluegrass.

During the Civil War the Nashville region had remained always a Mother Earth to many of the troops now gathered on Winstead Hill. The valley at Franklin was part of a vast limestone basin that encircled Middle Tennessee, with Nashville as a core. Sometime during the Paleozoic era, vast seas had covered the Middle Tennessee lands. Billions of sea creatures had died and were deposited into the ooze. Finally, some 300 million years ago, the waters receded, to display a thick, rich layer of limestone sediment wrought from the sea. Then some ancient geological eruption had taken place. A huge dome rose out of the region. Gradually the dome was weathered down in the process of millions of years; what was left was the rich bluegrass basin of Middle Tennessee, which by 1861 was considered one of the great breadbaskets of the Confederacy.

The basin was also a symbol of something denied. The Army of Tennessee had first tried at Shiloh to regain Mother Earth. Again they strove in the Kentucky campaign of 1862, but came to grief at the battle of Perryville. The invasion of Kentucky, for a time, did win back some of the coveted lands of Middle Tennessee, but not the bluegrass of Nashville and Franklin. Other battles would follow, in Tennessee and southward. It was part of a long retreat, and now, on a November afternoon, Hood's men were again close to Mother Earth.

But now the war was different. The men on the slopes below Franklin came from the mists of battle in Georgia. In Middle Tennessee, one resided in Federal territory. Nashville was the great dream of Hood and his men. But Nashville had been a Confederate city for only ten months before it had given tribute to the bluecoats of General Don Carlos Buell's army in late February 1862.

So much had changed in almost three years. Alfred Leland Crabb's "Nashville Gods" had vanished. The mighty landed estates from which much of the city's affairs had been controlled were not the same. The spacious grounds of Glen Leven, Belle Meade, and others were marked by Federal tents, entrenchments, or the naked stumps of felled trees. The railroad yards out present-day Broad

Street were alive with the activity of newcomers with boxcars of rations. The steamboat landings at the end of lower Broad Street brought thousands of other newcomers: soldiers, enterprising business folk, prostitutes, and others. Meanwhile, the city once considered the hub of the western Confederacy had been transformed into a huge, powerful Yankee fortress, with gun emplacements at forts such as Negley, Morton, and Casino. Factories hummed with the sound of machines, but the goods were intended for men who wore the blue.

And then, men who wore the gray appeared on the ridges south of Franklin. Truly they came almost as a ghost army, the remnant of men and legends raging larger than life. Once they had been in Franklin and Nashville, when the gray dreams were full. Now Tod Carter and his comrades out on the hill slopes were the very last.

★ ★ ★

Soon they would march down the slopes and across the bluegrass fields to Franklin. It did not require a West Point education to grasp that the task was almost impossible. Part of Schofield's entrenchments were clearly visible from the eminences of Winstead and Breezy hills. So, too, was the nature of the terrain over which Cheatham and Stewart must direct their men. In fact, Hood's men were really faced with two obstacles—the strength of the Federal line, and the peculiar qualities of the land between the two armies.

First, Schofield could have asked for no better defensive position. That morning his troops did not have to construct an entirely new line of fortifications. Most of the entrenchments had been prepared in 1862—1863 and were located within a peculiar curve of the Harpeth River. The Harpeth stream began in modern-day Rutherford County, not far from the community of Eagleville. Small creeks joined to form a river that journeyed over one hundred miles northwest to the Cumberland River below Nashville. The Harpeth was an old river traversing an ancient land. Near the present Confederate cemetery, off the Lewisburg Pike, stood the remains of a village of Mound Builders who had inhabited the bluegrass fields centuries earlier. In the late 1860s, Dr. Joseph Jones explored the remains of the Indian town. James A. Crutchfield, in his poignant book, *The Harpeth River: A Biography*, recaptures the excitement Jones felt. Here were the remains of earthworks almost four thousand feet in length and nine imposing burial and ceremonial mounds. Jones eagerly dug into the mounds and found precious remains such as a "Stone Sword" and copper plates— probably necklaces—with a cross in the middle of each.

For hundreds of years the Harpeth River had flowed on past the ancient earthworks, now crowned with the breastworks dug by other men. The river approached Franklin from the southeast. At a point approximately parallel to modern-day Cleburne and Stewart streets, the river curved first north, then east, and finally northwest again. Near the end of modern-day Margin Street, the river changed moods again and moved almost west and south. Finally, the fickle stream turned northeast again, in the vicinity of the modern-day Del Rio Pike.

All of this meant that Schofield's line was protected by the curves in the river, particularly on his left flank along the Lewisburg Pike. When the Federals arrived in Franklin on the morning of November 30, they quickly extended and enlarged the old earthworks present already, until the infantry line extended from the river east of town back to the stream northwest, along the present-day Hillsboro Road.

The most facile way to envision Schofield's line is to divide it into three units. On his left, between the modern Nashville and Lewisburg pikes, Schofield was heir to a strong line of works built previously in the war and improved substantially on November 30. This portion of the entrenchments began on the far left flank, where the river and Lewisburg pike ran parallel to a deep railroad cut in the Nashville and Decatur Railroad (present-day Louisville and Nashville Railroad). The line, located just north of the rail cut, led west from the river on an arc toward the Columbia Pike, slightly north of the site of the old Willow Plunge swimming pool, and the present-day Confederate cemetery. On an arc, Schofield's line followed a route parallel to the modern-day Cleburne and Stewart streets until it reached the Nashville-Columbia pike, present-day U.S. Highway 31, some 300 feet south of the Carter House.

On the far left, near the railroad and the Lewisburg Pike, any Confederate attack would have been difficult. First, the Confederates would be enfiladed by artillery posted across the Harpeth River. A powerful battery of guns was posted at Fort Granger, on the north bank of the river and just east of where the modern-day

Nashville Pike crosses that stream. Built in 1862 by General Gordon Granger, the fort once had housed over eight thousand men and two dozen guns. Prior to the battle of Franklin, the fort had been abandoned but was now reactivated. Captain Giles J. Cockerill had positioned Battery D, First Ohio Volunteer Light Artillery in the old fort. Other guns were placed by artillerymen of the Fourth and Twenty-third army corps on both sides of the Harpeth, on the extreme left of Schofield's line.

Other features gave good protection to the Federal left. The terrain southward to Winstead and Breezy hills was rolling but generally flat and open. Much of Schofield's front east of the Nashville-Columbia pike was covered with a thick hedge of Osage orange. The field commander, General Jacob Cox, made certain that his men cut down as much as possible in the time allowed and sharpened the branches into abatis. The remainder of the hedge served as a serious obstruction to any Rebel advance. Cox's division was the first to take position; the Yankee brigades, from left to right, were commanded by Colonel Israel N. Stiles, Colonel John S. Casement, and General James W. Reilly. Colonel Stiles reported that "substantial works were at once thrown up, and such portions of our front as were not already obstructed by a well-grown and almost impenetrable hedge were covered with a strong abatis made of the hedges which ran at right angles with the works." The Osage orange hedges, to which Stiles referred, were also used by Casement's brigade to construct an abatis across its front. In addition, Casement's strong earthworks were topped by headlogs with a three-inch space for rifles. Headlogs were also placed atop the works along the front of Reilly's brigade.

In the Federal center, there was one weak spot, at the critical place where the Nashville-Columbia road passed through the Federal works. Originally the road had been left open to allow the passage of traffic. On November 30, it remained open because Schofield had held General George D. Wagner's division to an advanced position, which will be described later.

The road crossing of Schofield's works was at once weak and strong. Certainly it boasted no breastworks replete with head-

---

View from Hood's command post on Winstead Hill, looking north across the ground where the Confederates charged the Federal line. ▶

[*Photograph by Rudy E. Sanders.*]

logs or deep outer ditch, as did the entrenchments to both sides of the pike. But there was protection. A retrenchment, fashioned in the manner of a barricade, stretched westward across the Nashville-Columbia road, some two hundred feet north of Schofield's breast-works east of the pike. The retrenchment extended due west direct-ly fronting the rear of the office and smokehouse of the Carter House property, and then bent back toward the northwest for some three hundred feet beyond the smokehouse. Behind this second work, Colonel Emerson Opdycke, on detachment from Wagner's advanced division, was posted.

General Jacob Cox, commanding here on the field, knew the vulnerability of the position and had reinforced it with massive artillery support. Actually three full artillery batteries were massed around the point where the road passed through Schofield's lines. West of the road, a battery was positioned just to the right of the smokehouse on the Carter property. A second battery was posi-tioned a short distance east of the pike, some two hundred feet south of the retrenchment, at the point where the main line of works crossed the pike. Today this battery site is located just north of the intersection of Cleburne Avenue and U.S. Highway 31, right below the Carter House. A third gun battery, slightly more ad-vanced, was located about three hundred feet east of the Columbia road. It was stationed in front of the cotton gin, which belonged to Fountain Branch Carter.

The presence at the Nashville-Columbia road of three full batteries was indicative of a strong position, but there was an added factor. Schofield's line angled in a peculiar fashion as it approached the Nashville-Columbia road from the east. As mentioned, the main line approached the pike parallel to the present-day Carter's Court shopping center, on a line parallel to Cleburne Avenue. But at a point 240 feet on the east side of the pike, Schofield's line bent back in a diagonal fashion until it reached the pike some 150 feet north of the entrenchments to the east. What this meant, of course, was that the gun battery at the cotton gin and the troops nearby could turn their weapons due westward and fire at any Confeder-ates who moved up the Columbia pike toward the Carter House.

Because the Union position at the center of the line, near the Carter house, became critical early in the engagement, and also because of the intense controversy engendered, General Cox's de-tailed description and explanations of that sector are especially

84   ]

valuable: "The cotton-gin formed a marked salient in the line," he said. "A little to the right of it the works made an angle toward the rear, coming back to join the epaulement of four guns on the left of the turnpike, ninety yards south of the Carter house. Where the line crossed the road, a gap was left of the full width of the road, for the continuous lines of wagons and artillery crowded it all the morning." On the west of the pike, Cox continued, the line extended "at right angles to the road for fifty yards on level ground, and then bent to the rear, descending the slope somewhat as it did so. This was the purpose of placing a battery on the summit at the right of the brick smokehouse, which could fire over the heads of the infantry in the front line. . . ."

Thus the middle sector of Schofield's line was as strong as the left sector. This middle portion extended westward from the Nashville-Columbia road to the Carter's Creek Pike. For several hundred yards it paralleled present-day Strahl Street west of the Nashville road and then curved to the northwest to strike the Carter's Creek Pike near present-day Eleventh Avenue South, where a grove of locust trees and a smaller fruit orchard fronted the Yankee works. The soldiers cut much of this down to make an abatis in front of their earthworks. The battery positioned just west of the Carter home afforded good protection, as did guns sprinkled at other positions along the line. Stationed here were the two brigades of Ruger's division, Colonel Silas A. Strickland on the left and Colonel Orlando H. Moore on the right. "I caused the line of breastworks to be made in the form of a broken line," said Ruger, "thus . . . giving a cross-fire on portions of the ground in front" of the division.

The third sector of the Federal line extended on a curve from the Carter's Creek Pike to the Harpeth River northwest of the town. The works extended in an arc from the Carter's Creek Pike across the present-day West Main Street and then curved back to the west and north to strike the Harpeth River near the present intersection of the Hillsboro and Del Rio pikes.

This was obviously the weakest portion of the Federal line. It lacked any works constructed in former times, as reported by General Walter C. Whitaker, who commanded a brigade positioned on the far right in the region of the present-day Hillsboro Pike. Whitaker said that his front line was endeavoring to construct a line of works but that it was "but half finished" when the Con-

federates attacked. Stationed on Whitaker's left flank was the brigade of Colonel Isaac M. Kirby, and farther to the east, near the
Carter's Creek Pike, General William Grose's men were "vigorous-
ly" at work "making barricades" when the storm erupted. Other
Federal officers recalled later the weakness of Schofield's right wing
between the Carter's Creek Pike and the river. Colonel John Bennett's infantry of the Seventy-fifth Illinois Regiment were kept hard
at work digging rifle pits. In fact, Hood's assault interrupted their
work. Bennett's men were ordered to drop their intrenching tools
and "take their places behind the uncompleted works. . . ."
Another Illinois regiment had tried to dig in, but an officer remembered there was "no time . . . to construct works of sufficient
strength to resist artillery before the enemy attacked."

Whether Hood knew of the actual weakness of this part of
the Federal line is in doubt. Later in the afternoon, General William
Bate's division would attack this portion. In his official report, Bate
noted, "The works to the left of the Carter Creek turnpike were not
strong, and with a vigorous assault should have been carried; a fact,
however, not known until the next day." Moreover, Hood's orders
for Bate's movement given via corps commander Cheatham, did
not contain *any* plans for fighting west of the Carter's Creek Pike.
In fact, Bate was supposed to align his left brigade along the east side
of the pike.

If Hood had taken the time for proper reconnaissance, the
weakness of this portion of Schofield's line would have been developed. There is little doubt that the condition of that sector could
not have been seen from Winstead Hill. The distance from the hill to
the closest point of the main Federal works was over two miles, on
an almost direct line along the Nashville-Columbia road to the
position of the Federals just south of the Carter house. On a direct
line, the view from the hill to Schofield's far right was a good three
miles. In addition, a range of hills and ridges, averaging 900 feet in
elevation, juts northward into the Franklin valley from the Winstead Hill range. Its size no doubt hindered Hood's visual reconnaissance.

Even if Hood had known of the weakness on the Union's far
right, he probably would not have altered his plans. Too much
frustration had built up within the tragic figure by the time he
reached Winstead Hill—memories of ambitions gone wrong at

Atlanta, of Sally Preston in Richmond, of the reality of the unhealed stump, of the debacle of Spring Hill.

Actually, Hood possessed three attack options at Franklin. First, he could have assailed the weak Federal right, but there is scant evidence that was even considered. Second, Hood could have employed broad flanking movements of the type suggested by Forrest. The evidence is substantial that Hood knew the flanks were open to such a maneuver. Around 3 P.M., a last council of war met on Winstead Hill at Hood's headquarters. Observers have given testimony that Hood understood that Schofield was vulnerable to a broad strategic maneuver on the flanks. General John C. Brown recalled later that Hood admitted that the immediate Federal center was very strong while the flanks were weak. But Hood insisted that if he tried to turn Schofield's flank, Schofield would retreat to Nashville. As Howell and Elizabeth Purdue observed in their *Pat Cleburne: Confederate General*, such reasoning was faulty. The nature of the open terrain on both banks of the river was such that Hood's cavalry and infantry could both have encircled Schofield. However, Hood, in his official report, maintained that a flanking move was "inexpedient," and "I therefore determined to attack him in front, and without delay."

The words *without delay* underscored Hood's third option. Simply, Hood intended to attempt to destroy Schofield's army with a massive headlong assault, leaving Schofield no room for retreat. At Gettysburg, Lee would have been grateful had General George Meade withdrawn from the field. Bragg at Chickamauga sought a flanking attack that would isolate General William Rosecrans from Chattanooga. At Shiloh, General Albert Sidney Johnston strove for another flanking thrust that would have driven General Ulysses Grant's men away from the Tennessee River. Hood wanted something else.

He said as much that afternoon, in the last council on Winstead Hill. Lieutenant L.H. Mangum had been a faithful member of General Patrick Cleburne's staff since the early days. He listened that afternoon as Hood gave Cleburne his final instructions, remembered them, and later recalled them. Cleburne's men were not to fire until General George Wagner's advanced line had been broken. They were to pursue the retreating advance to the main Federal line, then fix bayonets, go over the entrenchments, and break the enemy's line at all hazards. Here was the clue to what Hood intended, something he admitted on the first two pages of a chapter in his bitter memoir, *Advance and Retreat*. There is no doubt that Hood believed that attack was a means of discipline. Back on the Atlanta front, he had repeatedly rebuked the Army of Tennessee for what he considered cowardice. Hood stated openly that the army had become too cautious because the men had become accustomed to the protection of breastworks erected by General Joseph Johnston. Hood even suggested that the western army lacked the will to fight which he remembered existing in Lee's army. In his memoir, Hood spoke of the mortification that pervaded the ranks, suggesting the men were ashamed of timid conduct at Spring Hill; conduct fashioned by their association with Johnston's fortifications. There would be no more of that. Hood was determined that this army would show its mettle. In that last conference on Winstead Hill, Hood's twisted dreams clouded his logic. As Hood himself recalled, Cheatham and Stewart were given direct orders to drive Schofield into the Harpeth River at all hazards.

The concept of a frontal assault was little more than what General Daniel C. Govan later characterized it, something mad and haphazard. Even so, Hood did not do those things that might have given the assault even a slight hope for overall success. First, he refused to await the arrival of the remainder of the army—he was lacking one of his three infantry corps and all artillery save two batteries. Second, as Cheatham's and Stewart's men filed into position, it should have been obvious to Hood that he had not positioned the army to accomplish his objective, to break the center of the Union line.

Actually three separate, disjointed battles would be fought that day by Hood's infantry. On the far left, General William Bate's division was ordered to move through a gap in the Winstead Hill range, reach the Carter's Creek Pike, and subsequently move against the Federal works from the pike eastward. He was to be supported by General James Chalmers's cavalry division and a small part of another cavalry brigade led by General Jacob Biffle. This was, by far, and as previously noted, the weakest segment of Hood's line, and indicated his ignorance of the opportunities available on that flank.

Hood was more concerned with the center, but again he did

not align his men in a fashion to promote success. The ground available to deploy men on the west side of the Nashville-Columbia road was constricted because of the massive range of hills jutting northward into the Franklin valley. Still, only a solitary division of Cheatham's corps, that led by General John C. Brown, moved forward on the west side of the pike. Brown's division was aligned with two brigades on the front line, those of Generals States Rights Gist and George W. Gordon, with two in the second line, commanded by Generals John C. Carter and Otho F. Strahl. This line was weak. Brown's two-brigade front had to cover a battleline one-half mile in width, with only two reserve brigades.

The remainder of the center was in worse condition. Hood's great hope for smashing the Federal center depended upon two solitary divisions, which were to advance along both sides of the Nashville-Columbia pike. Brown was to the west, while General Patrick Cleburne would move on the east side of the pike. East of the road, the terrain was different from that on Brown's sector. In the Winstead Hill vicinity, where the army formed, the front was extremely wide. Flatlands stretched for almost two full miles eastward to the Harpeth River, a wide expanse to be covered by Cleburne's division and Stewart's thin corps.

Cleburne had absolutely no reserve on hand. His lines were stretched to the breaking point even before the attack began. General Hiram B. Granbury's brigade occupied the left, General D.C. Govan's command was in the center, while General Mark P. Lowrey's brigade was to extend the line eastward to the Nashville and Decatur Railroad (present-day Louisville and Nashville Railroad). Hood's ambition was to break the Federal center, in the area where Cheatham's divisions led by Generals John C. Brown and Cleburne must attack. Together they possessed only seven brigades out of the total of eighteen infantry brigades that Hood had on the field.

On the right wing came the greatest waste of strength. While Bate would advance in a solitary fashion along the Carter's Creek Pike and Brown and Cleburne would combine to strike the center, General Alexander P. Stewart's corps was assigned the entire right wing. The Confederate line in the Winstead Hill region stretched four and one-half miles from the Carter's Creek Pike to the Lewisburg road. Hood assigned the seven brigades of Stewart's corps to cover a front from the railroad to the Lewisburg Pike, a distance of a mile and a half. Meanwhile, two full cavalry divisions, commanded by Generals William H. "Red" Jackson and Abraham Buford, would cover the brief span between the Lewisburg Pike and the Harpeth River.

Again, this spread of manpower would come to haunt General Hood. On Bate's front, the far left, there were only a solitary infantry division and one cavalry division. On the right, Stewart and Forrest combined boasted five divisions. At the critical point along the Nashville-Columbia Pike, the two divisions of Brown and Cleburne had no reserves. Such were available—the three divisions in General Stephen Lee's corps. But Hood would not wait.

★ ★ ★

SOMEWHERE in Franklin a town clock moved forward toward four o'clock in the afternoon. The day had been bright and warm, a welcome respite from the sharp frosts and early snows of opening winter that had pestered Hood's thinly clad troops. Until shortly after the noon hour, the Confederate approach to Winstead Hill had been slowed by the last stand of Schofield's rearguard, the division of General George Wagner. Then by 1 P.M. Wagner had withdrawn northward along the pike to a second position on Merrill Hill. This small, rocky knob, which stands some one hundred feet above the surrounding valley, is approximately a mile north of Winstead Hill, west of the Columbia pike.

Then, by 3 P.M., Wagner moved his division northward again to Privet Knob, a position some one-half mile south of the main Federal works, on the west side of the present-day Nashville-Columbia pike, just south of the roadbed of the Louisville and Nashville Railroad. Lane's brigade occupied this high ground, while Conrad's brigade extended the advance line across the east side of the road.

Merrill Hill was abandoned now, and a moody General Patrick Cleburne rode forward to the overlook. Cleburne borrowed a telescope from a sharpshooter's Whitworth rifle and surveyed the terrain.

What did the Irishman see in this last glimpse before the regiments moved forward with bands playing? By one account, he made comment upon the massive strength of the Federal entrenchments. Perhaps he glimpsed the open nature of the ground in the center, where he and General John C. Brown must lead their men. It was rolling country with few trees and almost no fences. Federal artillery had a sweeping view of the field.

To his right, perhaps Cleburne could view the open terrain across the railroad, where General A.P. Stewart's corps must advance. Somewhere out there were the Osage orange hedge and the sharpended abatis that Stewart must encounter. And to the east, there was the meandering Harpeth River, which would curve to the northwest, forcing Stewart's center and right divisions to change front in a flanking march under galling artillery fire.

Then Cleburne returned to his own men waiting on the hill, with their fixed bayonets and the regimental bands awaiting the signal to play "The Bonnie Blue Flag." Soon someone would signal for the advance across the Indian summer fields, and the ghost of the once-mighty Army of Tennessee would come. They were the last, the very last.

# 5 /

# The Most Critical Moment

THE TIME was approaching four o'clock. Looking south across the broad, gently rolling plain toward Winstead Hill, the Federals anxiously waited. Intently they watched from behind hastily improved breastworks, suspenseful but fascinated by the precision and color of the spectacular military pageant unfolding before them.

In near perfect alignment advanced the imposing Confederate array. Well over one hundred regiments strong they came, bands playing, bayonets flashing, and scores of tattered battle flags flying in the late afternoon sun. General and staff officers and couriers were riding in front of and between the lines. The infantry moved at a quick step, and the artillery (one battery accompanying each corps) were brought forward in the intervals at a gallop, unlimbering and firing as soon as within range. "The sight inspired every man," discerned Colonel Ellison Capers of the Twenty-fourth South Carolina Infantry, "with the sentiment of duty."

It was an unforgettable martial display. Although Confederate manpower, as previously noted, was poorly deployed and probably inadequate under any circumstances to carry formidable defenses by frontal assault, nevertheless, it is an arresting fact that the Confederates were attacking in greater numbers than in the famous charge on the last day at Gettysburg or the well-known assaults against the "Hornets' Nest" at Shiloh. The onslaught would be, in a war where the Rebels bled themselves nearly to death by attacking, the last great Confederate charge of the whole bloody conflict. The enthralling scene of deployment and advance seemed like a grand prelude, an eerie death-dance, preceding a macabre holocaust in which soon the ghastly faces of the dead would graphically depict the hell of war.

"Spell-bound with admiration," a Yankee officer gazed southward, reflecting that "in a few brief moments . . . all that orderly grandeur would be changed to bleeding, writhing confusion, and that thousands of those valorous men of the South, with their chivalric officers, would pour out their life's blood . . ." All along the Union line soldiers watched tensely, some in fear, some in awe; many with a steely resolve to hold their position, still others in almost disbelief at what they saw occurring.

Many Federals found it hard to accept that the Confederates were actually making a frontal assault. Hours earlier, if the Rebels had been in position when the nervous Yankees, working as rapidly as tired bodies would permit, were still throwing up entrenchments and deploying their units, an attack would have seemed plausible. By noon, however, much of the apprehension of the Federal troops had been relieved. All the soldiers were in, except George Wagner's rear guard, still skirmishing in the distance beyond Winstead Hill with the Confederate advance. The Columbia Pike, which had been crowded most of the morning with double lines of wagons coming in, was empty and relatively quiet following the rattling of wheels and the clatter of picks and shovels. The troops at the breastworks had finally been able to get a little rest. Many of them were too tired to prepare any food, simply snacking on crackers and raw bacon, afterward dozing in the sun, the day being unseasonably warm for the last of November.

Schofield had been in town since dawn, organizing and developing an all-round bridgehead defense in a bend of the Harpeth River which loops around Franklin, enclosing the town on the east and north. Schofield neither intended nor wanted to fight at Franklin. He would have been across the Harpeth and well on his way to Nashville before Hood came in sight, except that when he arrived with his two lead divisions in the march from Spring Hill, under Cox and Ruger, the Union commander found that the turnpike bridge had been wrecked by the rising river and a second bridge partially destroyed by fire. Two days ago, anticipating a potential problem, he had urgently requested General Thomas, to send pontoons from Nashville, but these had not arrived and the ford was hardly passable.

Regardless of how imperturbable Schofield may have appeared (or seemed later when he wrote his memoir, *Forty Six Years in the Army*), he had to be worried. General Jacob Cox noted that he spoke with "a deep earnestness of feeling which he rarely showed." The Union commander had made a decision to throw up a line of field works and fight, if the Confederates forced him, with a river at his back, thus hoping to save his long wagon train—and hoping also, of course, to avoid embarrassment. Placing Cox in charge of the front line, Schofield told him to have the two divisions dig in astride the Columbia Pike, Cox's own division (temporarily commanded by General James W. Reilly) on the left and Ruger's division on the right, about half a mile south of the town, while awaiting the arrival of the three divisions still marching on the pike from Spring Hill. The wagons, which were already beginning to come in, would be parked in the cross streets of Franklin, leaving open the main thoroughfare.

Schofield then determined what could be done to improve the means of crossing the Harpeth. The approaches to the ford first received attention, the banks on both sides of the river being scraped to make the grade practicable for heavily laden army wagons. The engineers floored the railroad bridge with planks ransacked from nearby houses and constructed approaches for the wagons. Work was also begun on the old wagon bridge, as the main posts, still firmly grounded, were sawed off at the water's edge and new cross beams and stringers were attached and planked over. Although the bridge was intended only for the passage of troops, it was discovered that wagons, if care were taken, might also cross. By late morning a number of wagons had been crossed over the river. Too, of course, Schofield had ordered Captain Giles J. Cockerill's battery of three-inch rifled guns to the north bank at Fort Granger. The bastioned earthwork, located approximately a mile or a little more from where the Union line was being formed, was in position to command an enemy approach along the railroad cut, or generally from the south and east. Other cannon were parked nearby.

Meanwhile, General Cox had been deploying the Federal troops south of the town. At various times, as previously noted,

Site of General Schofield's headquarters.
*[Photograph by Rudy E. Sanders.]*

Franklin had been occupied by Union soldiers and entrenchments thrown up on the southern outskirts, but these had been partially obliterated and needed to be improved and strengthened by Cox's men. The entire Federal line, which would extend from the river and railroad on the left to the river on the right, would cover a position about two miles in length, strengthened by strategically placed artillery, all the guns positioned at intervals to blast an assaulting enemy head-on, while several guns could sweep a large circuit and rake a charging column from the flank as well. Perhaps, considering artillery power and angles of fire, the line should have been strongest in the center, where it crossed the Columbia Pike just south of the comfortable brick farmhouse owned by Fountain Branch Carter, which stood hardly fifty feet west of the Pike, facing toward the east.

From the river southward, the land rises slowly for a mile, reaching an elevation at the Carter house, which is about forty feet above "the square" in the heart of Franklin. The open fields lying south of the Carter house, and south of the long, rough curve of Federal entrenchments, are so slightly rolling as to appear almost flat. But actually they slope away, in Cox's words, "very gently from the line," and "along the whole front" of the Yankee position, continuing for more than a mile and a half to the Winstead Hill. Only a few farm buildings, with orchards here and there in the distance, blocked the vision in any direction. "Very few battlefields of the war," discerned a Federal officer, "were so free from obstruction to the view." Doubtless many Confederates would have agreed, although soon, once the battle had begun, a heavy pall of gunsmoke settled over the plain, obscuring the vision of all.

While Cox prepared the defensive front south of the town, Schofield was casting nervous glances toward his eastern flank. Upstream and to the left of the Federal line the Harpeth River was fordable at several places, and Schofield expected Hood, if anything, to attempt a flanking attack from that direction. The Union commander was at last in touch with his cavalry again, General Wilson operating some two and a half or three miles to the east on the road toward Triune. Instructing Wilson to cover the army's immediate flank and rear, Schofield assigned General Thomas J. Wood's division to the north bank of the river, near the fort, along with most of General Stanley's Fourth Corps artillery. That way, Wood's infantry could move quickly to assist Wilson's troopers in repelling any Confederate flankers.

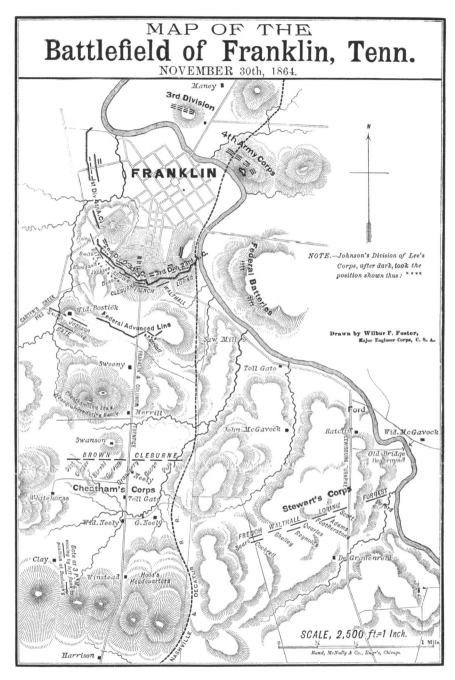

MAP OF THE
# Battlefield of Franklin, Tenn.
NOVEMBER 30th, 1864.

MAP 4. FRANKLIN.

Shortly before two o'clock, Wilson reported "Rebel infantry approaching Hughes' Ford, three miles above Franklin, apparently with the intention of crossing." A little later Wilson cautioned Schofield again, reporting that "Citizens say they can cross anywhere." These and other dispatches from Wilson gave Schofield good reason to believe that Hood would attempt to place a portion of his infantry across the river two or three miles to the east. This was what Schofield feared most—and apparently fully expected. Around three o'clock, he sent a telegram to General Thomas at Nashville explaining the situation as he understood it. Hood, said Schofield, "now has a large force, probably two corps, in my front, and seems preparing to cross the river. . . .I think he can effect a crossing tomorrow . . . and probably tonight, if he attempts it. A worse situation than this for an inferior force," continued the anxious Federal commander, "could hardly be found. . . . I have just learned that the enemy's cavalry is already crossing."

Probably it was Schofield's fear that Hood would launch a flanking attack—and some kind of flanking movement was the most sensible course for the Confederate commander—which explains Schofield's advance positioning of the last of his five divisions tramping in from Spring Hill, that of General George Wagner. Weary from the Spring Hill fight, then an all-night vigil against an attack, followed by a morning skirmish-march as rear guard of the army, Wagner's division took position astride the pike, but in front of the main Federal line, to better observe Hood's movements. This was about two o'clock. If one were looking south from the Carter house, a depression in Wagner's front and some scattered trees partially veiled Hood's lines, although there was a clear view from Stiles's brigade on the left of the main line. In the seemingly unlikely event of an enemy assault, Wagner's division was to fall back within the main works. If a flank movement developed, however, Wagner's division could rapidly swing eastward and help check Hood until reinforcements arrived. Actually, only two of the division's three brigades were deployed in the advanced position, Conrad's unit on the left of the pike, except for one regiment, which was on the right, along with all of Lane's brigade.

When Opdycke's brigade, the last to withdraw, approached the position occupied by Conrad and Lane, General Wagner rode forward and ordered Opdycke into line with them. Strenuously

Colonel Opdycke objected, declaring, so reported a Federal, that "troops out in front of the breastworks were in a good position to aid the enemy and nobody else!" Also, he pleaded that his brigade was "worn out" and entitled to a little rest. While discussing the matter, the two officers rode along the pike together, the brigade marching behind, until they reached the main line which, of course, was already fully occupied by other troops. About two hundred yards inside the breastworks, and north of the Carter house, they came to a sufficiently large, clear space and at last halted. There Wagner turned to ride away, with a final remark to the effect that, "Well, Opdycke, fight when and where you damn please; we all know you'll fight." The brigade stacked arms and fell out on the ground.

Certainly Opdycke's men were not the only Federals trying to recuperate. "There was now a period of rest and refreshment for the officers and men of the main line," recalled General Cox. The Yankee soldiers had hardly rested since they crossed Duck River on the night of November 27. "Our camp dinner over," Cox continued, "the tents at my headquarters were struck, the baggage packed, the wagons sent into town to fall in at the rear of the trains when the rest should be over the river. Our horses were fed and saddled, and the group of orderlies lounged on the grass by the roadside . . ., while the officers were sitting in the veranda of the house, smoking or sleeping, as the mood took them."

General Cox had commandeered the Carter home early in the morning, riding to the house and awakening the family to tell them that he must use a part of their home for his headquarters. Cox could not have known that the Carter house and its closely adjacent outbuildings would be standing over a century later—still bearing the marks of bullets to be fired that day—restored and preserved as a historic landmark to commemorate a battle in which he would soon participate, but avowedly did not expect. The red brick structure was simple but impressive. Over fifty feet in length across the front, the house had a centered double door (in an eight-panelled Colonial pattern), flanked by Doric columns and topped by a fanlight transom, the entrance complemented by a large window positioned to each side. The two ends of the house, distinguished by stepped parapet walls, culminated with chimneys at the top; the whole edifice conveyed a pleasing sense of balance and proportion. The homestead seemed to indicate an owner of substance, although it was modest compared to "Carnton," the house of Colonel Randall McGavock off to the southeast, or the "Harrison house," just south of the Winstead Hills, or "Everbright," the widow Rebecca Bostick's home a short distance to the southwest.

Sixty-seven-year-old, Virginia-born, Fountain Branch Carter, merchant, surveyor, and farmer, had spent most of his life in Tennessee, living for more than thirty years on the property astride the Columbia Pike. According to the 1860 census, he owned twenty-eight slaves and his real estate was valued at $37,000 and his personal estate at $25,000. Three of his sons, as previously noted, had enlisted in Company H, Twentieth Tennessee Infantry, soon after the war began. The youngest, Tod Carter, was then within sight of his home for the first time in more than two years. The oldest, Moscow, a colonel when captured in 1862, had been paroled and was at home with his father on this fateful November day.

Also present with the father and the paroled colonel, according to General Cox's account, were four daughters and a daughter-in-law. "Three families of young grandchildren were also in the house," he said, "and a couple of female servants, making a household of seventeen souls." (Besides these, a neighboring family of five would seek protection behind the stout brick walls when the battle began.) Naturally apprehensive for the safety of so many people, Mr. Carter had asked General Cox whether the family should leave the house. Believing that Hood would make a flanking movement rather than a frontal attack, Cox advised him not to leave unless it became certain that "a battle was imminent." The family clearly would not be molested, said Cox, while the headquarters tents were in the yard, but if the house was abandoned, he could not answer for the safety of its contents. Also, Cox added, according to his account, "if there were to be a battle, the very focus of it would certainly be there, and it would be no place for women and children." Colonel Moscow Carter likewise believed that Hood would not attack, and therefore the family decided to stay in the house.

Schofield, meanwhile, was anticipating the transfer of his troops across the Harpeth at dark. Shifting his headquarters north of the river to the house of Alpheus Truett, located on the east side of the Nashville Pike, the Federal commander was within easy

Fountain Branch Carter.

100    ]

The Carter Cotton Gin, a landmark during the battle, referred to by many participants as they recalled the fighting in later years.

The Carter House, showing the back porch and a portion of the yard where much heavy fighting occurred.

[*Photograph by Rudy E. Sanders.*]

The Carter House.                    [*Photograph by Rudy E. Sanders.*]

riding distance of the vantage point at Fort Granger. About three o'clock he issued orders for the infantry to be withdrawn at night-fall. By then the Confederates had been in view for some time, advancing slightly, stopping, and correcting their lines at intervals. A soldier in the Twenty-sixth Ohio Infantry watched from his advanced position west of the Columbia Pike, observing that "one from a distance might easily imagine them out for drill or inspection or preparing for a grand review. It was an imposing sight." Scho-field did not visit the front line to see the spectacle; obviously not anticipating a frontal assault, he depended upon Cox to keep him informed if anything significant developed. And Cox later said, "None of us were quick to believe that a *coup de main* would be attempted." Stanley, who was now also on the north bank of the river with Schofield, did not expect an attack either. "Nothing," he wrote in his report, "appeared so improbable as that they would assault."

The same opinion was held by many of the Federal general officers. Schofield's position was formidable. Hood had not been willing to attack fortified lines at Columbia. Now, with the trains in and the troops entrenched, and the strength of the Federals well over 20,000, perhaps 25,000, an assault did not make any sense—or so the Union officers thought. Men who may have been worried earlier had relaxed and become more confident that the Rebels were not likely to do anything more than put on a colorful show. And then, little more than a half hour before sunset, they saw the Confederates coming.

Eighteen infantry brigades moved across the open plain, Stewart's corps on the east side of the Columbia Pike and Cheatham's corps on the west, except for Cheatham's right flank under Cleburne, which was advancing east of the pike. General Cox, watching from a knoll in the rear of Stiles's brigade, where he had the best view of the whole field, said that "when the Confeder-ates . . . started forward, no more magnificent spectacle was ever witnessed." Another who recorded his impressions was Adam Weaver, One Hundred and Fourth Ohio, near the Carter cotton gin, composing a letter to "Charlotte." Now he quickly wrote that he heard his captain remark to a lieutenant, "Do you think the Lord will be with us today?" Silently Weaver said a prayer and con-cluded: "I must close out this letter, as we are ordered up to our positions. One last look south. The air is hazy. I can hear bands playing. . . ."

Schofield was riding with Stanley from the Truett house toward the river when he received the news that the enemy was assaulting. Stanley galloped toward the front to take command of his troops, while Schofield turned off to the left and rode to the fort. Several Union veterans would later criticize the Federal commander for remaining on the north bank of the Harpeth at the fort, rather than assuming personal command on the line. "When Stanley started for the front, Schofield started for the rear," said one Yankee. Another wrote that he was "well beyond the range of every rebel bullet that was fired," and still another veteran bitterly remarked that the general "possessed the 'rascally virtue called caution' in an eminent degree" and was never known to "be reckless enough to expose his carcass to the fire of the rebels."

Whether or not deserved for actions at some other time, these criticisms of Schofield make no sense at Franklin. If Hood were attempting to flank him—which Schofield doubtless still expected—the fort was the logical place for the Federal commander, even if a simultaneous assault were being made on the front line. The latter would be the responsibility of Cox and Stanley. Fort Granger was very close to the planked-over railroad bridge, which enabled Schofield to communicate with Cox's headquarters, only a little over a mile away. The fort overlooked the left half of his front line, readily visible with field glasses, while also affording a view for some distance to the flank and rear. From there he could best see the overall picture, determine what was developing, and, as Cox summarized, "where alone he could see the cavalry . . . on the left where Forrest and Wilson were . . . engaged."

On came the Confederates. Weapons loaded and bayonets fixed, they grimly marched toward the Yankees. Some soldiers noticed the flurries of rabbits and the whirring coveys of quail escaping the tramping feet of the steadily moving Rebels. The Federals waited and endured. The tension mounted. In fact, the stress was nearing the panic level in Wagner's two advanced brigades astride the Columbia Pike, out in front of the main Union line.

"We had all supposed," explained John K. Shellenberger, a Federal company commander in Conrad's brigade east of the pike, that the advanced position "would be only temporary, but . . . an orderly came . . . with instructions . . . to hold the position to the last man, and to have my sergeants fix bayonets and to instruct my company that any man, not wounded, who should . . . leave the line without orders, would be shot or bayonetted by the sergeants." Veteran soldiers, said Shellenberger, comforted themselves with the thought that such harsh orders were for the benefit of a new assignment of drafted men. "Never before had they received any such orders on going into battle."

Shellenberger continued his account, stating, "The opinion was . . . universal that a big blunder was being committed in compelling us to fight with our flank fully exposed in the midst of a wide field. . . . The indignation of the men grew almost into a mutiny and the swearing of those gifted in profanity exceeded all their previous efforts. . . ." Some men, their enlistments expired, were scheduled to be mustered out of service as soon as the army was back in Nashville. Among these was a first sergeant by the last name of Libey, who, when the Rebels were approaching, twice got up from the line and started for the breastworks, vehemently declaring something to the effect that he "would not submit to having his life thrown away, after his time was out, by such a stupid blunder," only to return upon the uncompromising order of his captain, "God damn you, come back here!" Just as he feared, the sergeant had only a few minutes to live.

Closer and closer came the Confederates—and the mental stress continued to build. About four hundred yards from Wagner's brigades, perhaps a half mile or more from the Federal breastworks, the columns halted, shifted smartly into a formation of two battle lines, and then charged, screaming as they plunged forward. A Confederate regimental commander in Brown's division, west of the Columbia Pike, vividly recalled the scene. "Just before the charge was ordered," said Colonel Ellison Capers, "the brigade passed over an elevation from which we beheld the magnificent spectacle the battlefield presented. . . . General [States Rights] Gist, attended by Captain H.D. Garden and Lieutenant Frank Trenholm, of his staff, rode down our front, and returning, ordered the charge, in concert with General [George W.] Gordon. In passing from the left to the right of the regiment the general waved his hat to

---

General States Rights Gist.

us, expressed his pride and confidence in the Twenty-fourth [South Carolina] and rode away in the smoke of battle, never more to be seen by the men he had commanded on so many fields." A thirty-three-year-old Charlestonian who had attended South Carolina College and Harvard Law School, Gist had seen action in Mississippi during the Vicksburg campaign, afterward leading either a brigade or a division throughout the Chattanooga and Atlanta campaigns.

Commanding another of Brown's brigades was General Otho French Strahl, a native Ohioan who had settled in Tennessee and was practicing law at Dyersburg when the war began. A veteran of Shiloh, Perryville, and Stones River, as well as Chickamauga, Chattanooga, and the Atlanta campaign, Strahl went into the fight on foot rather than on horseback, reportedly telling his men as he advanced with them, "Boys, this will be short, but desperate."

On pressed the charging Confederates. "They were coming on the run," a Yankee in Wagner's advanced position recalled, "emitting the shrill rebel yell, and so near that my first impulse was to throw myself flat on the ground and let them charge over us."

Closing with a rush, coming directly against the front and around the flanks of Wagner's two unfortunate brigades, was the weight of Cheatham's corps, the divisions of Cleburne and Brown. Cleburne's famed command, aggressive attackers at Shiloh and Stones River, staunch defenders of the Rebel right flank at Missionary Ridge, and veterans of numerous campaigns, swept forward on the right, or east, side of the Columbia Pike, while Brown's less renowned but effective unit was surging forward on the left. A native of Giles County, and a lawyer by profession, the thirty-seven-year-old John Calvin Brown, having survived capture at Fort Donelson and wounds at Perryville and Chickamauga, was to be severely wounded within a few minutes at Franklin, but would recover to become the first Democratic governor of Tennessee after the war.

Cleburne and Brown were immediately exposed to a galling fire from a section of artillery stationed with Wagner's brigades and soon subjected to volleys of infantry fire as well. But instead of halting the advancing Rebels, the rattling Yankee fusillade served

General Otho F. Strahl.

only to check them for a moment. Then they charged into the exposed Federal brigades. The Union artillery section was already gone, having limbered up at the last moment and retired within the main line, in accordance with orders sent to it by the chief of artillery.

Wagner, of course, had been ordered to withdraw his two advance units at the first indication of a general assault. The near disaster that resulted from the brigades' remaining in front of the Federal line cost Wagner his command within a week and became the subject of much controversy, as Wagner, Cox, Stanley, and Schofield all disavowed any blame for the blunder. Perhaps Wagner's brigade commanders were confused about what was expected of them, but even so, the primary responsibility was Wagner's. At the very least, he was careless; possibly guilty of bad judgment. Not present with the brigades, the general had set up headquarters in a grove of trees beside the pike north of the Carter house. The Rebel advance was well underway before he even knew that it had begun. Then, according to Cox, who stated his source was the testimony of two officers who were present with Wagner, that general, "in a moment of excitement, forgetting himself and his orders, sent back a command to fight."

Wagner denied it. One of three things must have occurred: the general never issued orders to retire in the event of an enemy assault, or his orders to withdraw were somehow not clearly understood, or perhaps thinking of his success the previous day at Spring Hill, he was moved by a vision of grandeur to imagine that he could again hold his ground. Because Wagner was neither with his units nor paying attention to what was developing, the general was at fault, whatever he did or did not do.

Brown and Cleburne quickly overran the advanced Federal brigades. From the Union side, W. A. Keesy of the Sixty-fourth Ohio, described the scene: "Our orderly sergeant," said Keesy, was "calling very imploringly to the captain: 'Captain, for God's sake, let us get in behind the works. Why, just see them coming! Enough to swallow us up!' " But the captain's response was, "Sergeant, keep your place, sir, and not another word." Then Keesy recalled the sharp order ringing out: "Make ready, fire at will!" and suddenly all was "smoke, fire and the roar of battle." But soon was heard the command, "Fire, left oblique, boys! Fire, left oblique! They are bearing down on our left!" The Ohioan remembered that the scene was "a wall of blazing guns all along our line," as the men loaded and fired rapidly until, faintly above the din of battle, he heard the command to "Fall back!" The enemy, wrote Keesy, was upon us "in overwhelming numbers," and he turned and ran for the main line of works.

John Shellenberger also gave a vivid account of this action by the advanced Federal brigades: "The salient of our line was near the pike and there the opposing lines met in a hand-to-hand encounter in which clubbed muskets were used, but our line quickly gave way. I had been glancing uneasily along our line," confessed the officer, "watching for a break as a pretext for getting out of there," and was looking toward the pike when the break first started. It ran along the line so rapidly that it reminded me of a train of powder burning. I instantly sprang to my feet and . . . shouted to my company, 'Fall back! Fall back!' and gave an example of how to do it by turning and running for the breastworks. . . . While running rapidly with body bent over and head down," Shellenberger said he collided with a man running in the same crouched manner but headed at a different angle. "The shock was so great that it knocked him down and pretty well knocked the wind out of me. Just as we met, a rebel shell exploded close over our heads and as his body was rolling over on the ground, I caught a glimpse of his upturned face and, in its horrified look, read his belief that it was the shell that had hit him." That soldier was unharmed, but First Sergeant Libey's strong premonition of death was realized; racing for the comparative safety of the main Federal line, he was shot and killed instantly.

Both Federal brigade commanders, Lane and Conrad, said in their After Action Reports that they retired only when each had found that the other's brigade was falling back. If anything, such testimony indicates that both began retiring at approximately the same moment. Certainly neither held his ground very long. Watching from the Federal breastworks, just west of the pike, a captain in the Seventy-second Illinois simply observed that the two brigades "gave way on the approach of the enemy and rushed pell-mell into our works."

Apparently all of Wagner's Federals were not able to flee back to the main line quite so readily—even if Confederate fire did not bring them down. Colonel Lane reported that his command "had much difficulty in getting into the works, owing to a heavy line of abatis of locust boughs placed there for some purpose, through which my line had to pass." Seemingly a brigade commander would know the purpose of abatis, but however that may have been, his problem was real, as confirmed by Confederate Colonel Capers's After Action Report.

On pressed the charging line of Gist's brigade, said Capers, "driving the advance force of the enemy pell-mell [obviously a word favored by both sides] into a locust abatis, where many were captured and sent to the rear; others were wounded by the fire of their own men. This abatis was a formidable and fearful obstruction. The entire brigade was arrested by it. Fortunately for us the fire of the enemy slackened to let their advance troops come in, and we took advantage of it to work our way through."

For those Yankees not troubled by the abatis, it was a footrace with the Rebels to the Federal main line, the pursuing attackers clubbing and shooting the terrified Federals as they fled. One of Cleburne's command, Captain Samuel T. Foster, Twenty-fourth Texas Cavalry (dismounted), entered a description of the action in his diary. "As soon as they break to run our men break after them. They have nearly one half mile to run to get back to their next line—so here we go right after them and yelling like fury and shooting at them at the same time. Kill some of them before they reach their works, and those that are in the [main] line of works are not able to shoot us because their own men are in front of us—and between us and them."

On the west side of the pike was a private in the First Tennessee Regiment of General John C. Carter's brigade. From the viewpoint of Sam R. Watkins, who began by saying, "Would to God that I had never witnessed such a scene," the charge was re-created in the following words: "As we marched through an open field toward the rampart of blood and death, the Federal batteries began to open. . . . 'Forward, men,' is repeated all along the line. A sheet of fire was poured into our very faces. . . . 'Forward, men!' The air is loaded with death-dealing missiles. . . . I had made up my mind to die—felt glorious. . . . Cleburne's division was charging their works," said Watkins, perhaps indicating that the Irishman's division had slightly outdistanced Brown's. "I . . . got to their works," the private continued, "and got over on their [the Yankees'] side. But in fifty yards of where I was, the scene . . . seemed like hell itself. . . . Dead soldiers filled the entrenchments. . . . It was a grand holocaust of death. . . . I do not know who was to blame. . . ."

Perhaps the most polished and graphic Confederate account of the grand assault on the Federal center was penned by General George Gordon, commanding a brigade in Brown's division, who captured both the ecstasy and the misery of the spectacular episode. As the Yankees of Wagner's division fled toward their main line, Gordon said that "the shout was raised, 'Go into the works with them!' This cry was taken up and vociferated from a thousand throats," the general said, "as we rushed on after the flying forces we had routed—killing some in our running fire, and capturing others who were slow of foot—sustaining but small losses ourselves until we arrived within about one hundred paces of their main line and stronghold. . . ." There the Rebels were swept by a devastating fire from the Union ranks.

Continuing with an explanation, Gordon said that the Federals had "reserved their fire for the safety of their routed comrades who . . . were just in front of and mingled with the pursuing Confederates. When it became no longer safe for themselves to reserve their fire, they opened upon us (regardless of their own men . . .) such a hailstorm of shot and shell, musketry and canister, that the very atmosphere was hideous with the shrieks of . . . death." The din of thousands of small arms firing, joined by the roar of artillery and explosions of shells, mingled with the sounds of men shouting and yelling in their struggle for victory, General Gordon concluded, "all made a scene of surpassing terror and awful grandeur."

General Stanley claimed that the old soldiers in Wagner's brigade got away but the recruits were captured, being afraid to run under enemy fire. Clearly the veterans were not afraid to run, and some rushed straight down the pike, through the main line at the Carter house, and on into Franklin, never halting until they were winded or had reached the river bank. General Wagner, furious, tried to rally them, but was swept backward by the mass of men. Despite their desire to escape, several hundred were captured, and a Federal officer on the main line observed, "The triumphant Confederates, now more like a wild, howling mob than an organized army, swept on to the very works, with hardly a check from any quarter. So fierce was the rush that a number of the fleeing soldiers—officers and men—dropped exhausted into the ditch, and lay there while the terrific contest raged over their heads."

Some, however, were not permitted to stay. So it was with W.A. Keesy, who finally scrambled into the Federal main works, "helpless from exhaustion," as he phrased it. There a company captain soon tapped Keesy with his sword and told him to get out of the ditch. "I will not have my company demoralized by stragglers coming in here," said the captain. Climbing out of the ditch, Keesy scrambled another fifteen or twenty rods to the rear, taking precarious refuge "in a little hollow in the ground." From there he watched the Confederates pouring over the embankment, and later described what he saw: "On our right the artillery teamsters stampeded. The ammunition went with the teams and caissons, and the gunners took picks, shovels or anything at hand, and nobly defended the guns." One of the guns was loaded but, in the confusion caused by the stampede of the teamsters, had not been fired. The Confederates, thinking the battery had been silenced, made for the embrasure, and, Keesy said, "a large crowd was rushing to the muzzle of the gun. The man with the lanyards tremblingly held his fire until the first rebel in the rush placed his hands upon the muzzle of the cannon to spring over, when he let her go. Like a huge thunder bolt that awful roar and flash went blasting through that crowd of men, annihilating scores! Arms, legs and mangled trunks were torn and thrown in every direction."

Keesy also recorded his impressions of the fleeing Federals, as many raced for the town and the river. "Some Zouave officers, mounted and armed to the teeth, deployed across the pike and flourishing their swords and revolvers, swore terribly that they would shoot the first man who undertook to pass, but all was to no avail. The cyclone of bewildered humanity was not to be stayed in that way."

But even as the right and center of Cheatham's inspired corps vehemently bore down upon the Federals at the Columbia Pike—a potential triumph at hand if the Yankees' blunder with their advanced brigades could be effectively exploited—serious coordination problems had developed with the overall attack which may already have doomed to failure the desperate Confederate effort. The Rebel ranks of Brown's and Cleburne's divisions charging into the Federal entrenchments could not have been aware, and probably many of their general officers did not realize, that

Cheatham's left wing under Bate and part of Stewart's corps to their right were not converging on the enemy line in a simultaneous assault. With Rebel and Yankee strength rather closely matched, the Confederates could not afford such a disjointed attack. Yet, that was precisely what was occurring as Cleburne's and Brown's men poured through the gap on the pike near the Carter house, outdistancing any support on their left flank—and, of course, with no reserves to follow up and solidify a breakthrough. However, at the ominous moment when the animated Confederates surged into the enemy breastworks on both sides of the Columbia Pike, with a reckless élan, as if to defeat the Yankees at any cost, their chances of victory must have seemed good.

Confusion prevailed among many of the Federals at the point of penetration, as the Rebels not only broke through along the pike but also widened the gap by knocking a regiment loose from the breastworks on each side of the road. In fact, Cox reported, "most of Strickland's brigade broke from the first line." Soldiers in the trenches, disconcerted by the crowd trampling over them, confused by Wagner's officers calling upon their men to "rally at the rear" and supposing the order applied to them too, were carried away by the surging mass of sweaty, bloody humanity. Adding to the disorder were frightened horses galloping to the rear, carrying off the ammunition chests for the batteries near the pike, as the Rebels appeared on the breastworks, taking possession of the main Federal line on both sides of the road, the break extending from near the cotton gin on the east across Strickland's entire front on the west. They also seized eight guns, four on each side of the pike. Those on the east side, still loaded, were turned to fire on the Federal flank near the cotton gin.

Exhausted by his third-of-a-mile dash, John Shellenberger lay in the Federal entrenchment near the cotton gin when he spotted the cannon pointing toward him with a group of Confederates at the breech trying to fire into the Union flank. Not knowing that the bolting battery horses had carried away the primers in the ammunition chests, the terrified Federal said, "I . . . shut my eyes and set my jaws to await the outcome where I was lying." The cannon never fired, of course, the Rebels finding no way to set them off. If the Confederates had succeeded in firing the guns, the Yankee soldier speculated, "they would have widened the breach in our line so much farther to our left that it might have proved fatal, since the two brigades holding our line, from the vicinity of the cotton-gin to the river, had each but a single regiment of reserves. The men at my side, when I first saw the cannon, were so busily engaged in keeping out the rebels who filled the ditch on the other side of the parapet, that I do not believe they ever saw the . . . cannon posted to rake the ditch."

The battery of artillery placed in the salient angle at the cotton gin never fell to the Confederate drive, although the Rebels tried hard and continued to try to force a passage and several times succeeded in getting into the embrasure, pushing their guns through and firing upon the cannoneers. Lieutenant Aaron P. Baldwin, in command of the Yankee battery, told of the hand-to-hand conflict, saying that the enemy was "so unpleasantly close that we had to resort to the use of sponge-staves, axes and picks, to drive them back."

With their foothold at the Columbia Pike, the Confederates indeed seemed to threaten the whole Federal position. At that very moment, General Stanley was riding into the midst of a pall of acrid gunsmoke, awesome sound, and bloody destruction. "I arrived at the scene of disorder, coming from the town on the Columbia pike," he wrote. "The moment was critical beyond any I have known in any battle—could the enemy hold that part of our line, he was nearer to our two bridges than the extremities of our line. Colonel Opdycke's brigade was . . . about 100 yards in rear of the works. I rode quickly to the left regiment and called to them to charge; at the same time I saw Colonel Opdycke near the center of his line urging his men forward. I gave the colonel no order, as I saw him engaged in doing the very thing to save us, viz, to get possession of our line again."

The penetration of the Federal line by the hard-driving spearhead of Cleburne and Brown did not spread. Charging straight through the routed men to plug the gap came the brigade of Colonel Emerson Opdycke, a thirty-four-year-old Ohioan with a fiery reputation earned in most of the major western battles, from Shiloh, where he first led a charge; to Missionary Ridge, where his troops were among the first to reach the crest; to Resaca, where he was badly wounded but recovered in time to lead an assault up Kennesaw Mountain. Opdycke's men, some needing no orders, charged into the break, fighting hand-to-hand with the nearly exhausted Confederates, Opdycke himself setting a conspicuous example, first, according to one account, "firing all the shots in his revolver and then breaking it over the head of a rebel, snatched up a musket and fought with that for a club."

Captain Edward Bates, commanding the One Hundred and Twenty-fifth Ohio Regiment in Opdycke's Brigade, later described the rush to fill the breach near the Carter house. "The line at the works was broken," he said, and "a mass of frightened recruits and panic-stricken men came surging back," while "the clash of arms, the whizzing of bullets, and the demoniac yell of an elated foe was all that could be heard, when the order came from our leader to advance my regiment. . . ." Bates reported that "the One Hundred and twenty-fifth Ohio then charged double quick through and over crowds of routed men, and met the rebels at our abandoned works, and poured into them withering volleys that sent them reeling back . . . strewing their way with flags, dead and wounded."

Most Civil War battles, contrary to popular legend, involved little or no bayonet fighting. Franklin, however, combined some of the grisliest features of a frontal assault penetration and bayonet fighting in a general hand-to-hand melee. "The men fought like demons," wrote a Confederate, as they used "clubbed muskets and the bayonet." An Illinois Colonel reported, "It would be impossible to picture that scene in all its horrors. I saw a Confederate soldier, close to me, thrust one of our men through with the bayonet, and before he could draw his weapon from the ghastly wound, his brains were scattered on all of us that stood near, by the butt of a musket swung with terrific force by some big fellow whom I could not recognize in the grim dirt and smoke that enveloped us."

Opdycke himself, in a sometimes dramatic After Action Report, said "the battle raged with indescribable fury" and credited his men "when the . . . masses of the enemy had stormed and carried our main works at the keypoint of our whole position," with rushing "grandly and defiantly forward, your bayonets gleaming . . .," to assail "the victorious foe . . ., and saved the army from disastrous overthrow." Opdycke would be promoted to brigadier general for his part in this action at Franklin.

For all their fierce fighting, Opdycke's brigade had some help in sealing the breach at the pike—considerable help in fact. Colonel John S. White's Sixteenth Kentucky, in the second line of Reilly's brigade immediately east of the pike, was a major unit in

[ 117

stemming the Rebel onslaught. General Cox reported that "neither Colonel White . . . nor Colonel Opdycke waited for the word to charge, but were in motion before the order could reach them. White was nearest the parapet and reached it soonest. . . ." In a seemingly accurate, brief, After Action Report, White said: "Observing a portion of the line in my front give way, I ordered my regiment to charge the enemy, who were occupying the works so abandoned, which it did, engaging them in a hand-to-hand conflict, which lasted about forty minutes. I succeeded in driving them beyond the works, inflicting a heavy loss." Colonel White received a severe wound in the face but refused to leave the line while the struggle was so fierce.

The Federals who had fallen back from the line were being rallied by officers, and many returned to their posts to fight, mingling with those at the front until, in some places, Cox reported, there was "a wall three or four deep, those in the rear loading the muskets for those who were firing." Stanley was helping to rally these men, and remembered that he "heard the old soldiers call out, 'Come on, men, we can go wherever the general can.' " But in the midst of the action, Stanley's horse was killed, "and no sooner had I regained my feet," said the general, "than I received a musket-ball through the back of my neck. . . ." According to Cox, Stanley "was reluctantly persuaded to return to his quarters for surgical help."

Fighting was raging all about the Carter house, of course, where more than twenty people were huddled in the cellar seeking refuge. Mr. Carter gave an account of the battle as he experienced it from within those confines: "The cellar afforded the securest retreat, and hardly was it reached before the din of battle grew appalling. In the gloom of the cellar the children cowered at the feet of their parents, and while the bullets rained against the house, and a cannon ball went crashing through, all seemed in a state of acute expectancy, but gave no audible sound of fear."

The high tide of the Rebel advance had passed. In the face of savage counter-attack, the Confederates were slowly forced back, either to the main line of Federal works, or beyond. Cleburne's men, east of the pike and in front of the cotton gin, were driven back from the enemy line and pinned down, being decimated by a cross-fire. Federals from Casement's brigade to their right, raked Cleburne's men from the flank, some of the Yankees in the Sixty-fifth Indiana Regiment firing repeating rifles. "I never saw men put in such a terrible position as Cleburne's division was in for a few minutes," recalled James Barr of the Sixty-fifth Illinois. "The wonder is that any of them escaped death or capture," wrote this soldier who had the somewhat unusual experience of being captured by the charging Confederates, and then freed by the Federal countercharge. In addition to the repeating rifles in Casement's brigade, Cox mentions that two companies in the Twelfth Kentucky of Reilly's brigade were armed with "revolving rifles," and other troops are mentioned as having breech-loading rifles—weapons that could be fired much faster than the standard muzzleloaders.

West of the pike, part of Brown's division had madly rushed past the Carter house. Giving ground slowly and grudgingly, Brown's division was gradually pushed back. General Cox, in his book on the battle, said that "all the circumstances show that the gap west of the Carter house was longest open, and that bodies of the enemy got fartherest within our lines there." Cox was convinced that "the focus of the fight was around the position of the Forty-fourth Missouri, just in the rear of the Carter house. . . ." That regiment, he said, "had more men killed than all the other regiments of the brigade." Describing the intensity of the struggle near the Carter house, the Union line commander wrote that "the men in and about the Carter buildings were better covered than the rest. . . . They fired from the windows of the buildings and from every opening or interspace that could be used as a loop-hole. They clustered at the corners and between the out-buildings, and fired obliquely from this cover."

The men of Brown's division were finally thrust back to the breastworks over which they had stormed, but there they grimly held on and refused to retreat farther, forcing the Yankees to throw up a barricade across the Carter garden. Seizing upon fences and such material as was close at hand, the Federals constructed a new line and across the narrow interval the battle raged, neither side able to advance in the face of the other's withering fire. Brown's losses were appalling. "Confederate generals not only led their forces into battle, they died with their men," wrote Grady McWhiney and Perry D. Jamieson in their recent book, *Attack and Die*, stating that "fifty-five percent of all Confederate generals (235 of 425) were killed or wounded in battle." Before the fight was over, Brown's losses would be even greater than this average—seriously wounded himself, he would also lose all four of his brigade commanders: Gist and Strahl killed outright, Carter mortally wounded, and Gordon taken prisoner. On Brown's right, the Yankees from their regained works had an excellent field for enfilading fire, because of the angle in the line; on Brown's left, where Bate had not made connection, the Federals could also pour in a flanking fire.

Meanwhile, the assault by Stewart's corps on the right had not gone well. Apparently French's division on the left of Stewart's corps, encountering no major problems during the advance, struck the Federal line first—perhaps even slightly before the right wing of Cheatham's corps, Cleburne's division, which, of course, was briefly held up by Wagner's defenders. French went into action just east of the cotton gin, some men gaining the enemy breastworks, only to be quickly repulsed. Regardless of precisely when he hit the line, French clearly had been thrown back before Cleburne's division was compelled to retreat from the Yankee breastworks near the Columbia Pike.

The advance of the other divisions of Stewart's corps, Walthall in the center and Loring on the right, had been slowed by the curve of the Harpeth River, which flowed northwestward until it reached the flank of the Federal works near the railway cut at the Lewisburg Pike. Because of the course of the river, the width of the plain contracted rapidly as Stewart advanced, necessitating readjusting and changing the direction of his lines on the center and right. Additional delay occurred when Walthall and Loring struck the deep railroad cut. This, too, forced a change of front toward the left.

As the men scrambled around the railroad cut, they were struck by a murderous fire from a battery of guns masked on the opposite side of the river. As Stewart's soldiers swung to the left, their entire flank was exposed to this enfilading fire. A severe bombardment from the three-inch rifles in Fort Granger was also striking them, as was the fire of the battery stationed near the Lewisburg Pike. Then, as they struggled through the massive abatis in front of the parapets, they were met by a terrible small-arms fire. Walthall's division particularly suffered from the rapid fire of Yankee units armed with repeating rifles.

General Walthall's report conveys well the determination and savagery of the fighting and the appalling loss of life occurring in Stewart's Corps. "Both officers and men seemed fully alive to the importance of beating the enemy here at any cost, and the line moved steadily forward," he wrote. "There was an extensive, open, and almost unbroken plain . . . across which we must pass. . . . This was done under far the most deadly fire of both small-arms and artillery that I have ever seen troops subjected to," Walthall reported in his matter-of-fact style. "Terribly torn at every step by an oblique fire from a battery advantageously posted at the enemy's left, no less than by the destructive fire in front, the line moved on and did not falter till, just to the right of the pike, it reached the abatis fronting the works. Over this," said the division commander, "no organized force could go, and here the main body of my command, both front line and reserve, was repulsed in confusion; but over this obstacle, impassable for a solid line, many officers and men (among the former Brigadier General [Charles M.] Shelley) made their way, and some, crossing the ditch in its rear, were captured and others killed or wounded in the effort to mount the embankment. Numbers of every brigade gained the ditch and there continued the struggle. . . ."

Somewhere over to Walthall's right, one of the Rebels charging toward the Yankee line in Loring's division, Adams's brigade, was Captain William C. Thompson, Sixth Mississippi, from Simpson County, Mississippi. A veteran of numerous campaigns, Thompson had been among those charging up the rather steep hillside just south of Shiloh Church toward Sherman's division early on the morning of April 6, 1862, when he had been struck down in an attack that cost his regiment 300 casualties out of a force of 425 men. Just as in that awful fight, Thompson's unit was again being raked by enemy fire from the front and the right flank. "During our division attack," he wrote, "the Federals had a battery planted on the right of the . . . river that we could not reach. This battery damaged us severely, using canister. The Confederate troops were being mowed down. . . . At the same time the whole division was suffering from galling musketry fire by the enemy entrenched in our immediate front."

Continuing his account, the captain said that "just after the three brigades combined, and in the midst of the enemy artillery fire, I was shot through the right leg. The ground about me was covered with the fallen. I managed with the assistance of the litter men to get to a point where the bullets were not flying so thick. I remained there for the remainder of the night, suffering great pain. . . ." Actually, compared to his brother, William Thompson was fortunate. Captain Arthur J. Thompson, Seventh Mississippi Infantry, lost his leg just below the knee, besides suffering other wounds, in the same bloody struggle at Franklin.

Across the way in the Union lines, looking south from the breastworks on the left flank, between the river and the Lewisburg Pike, was Colonel Israel N. Stiles. His brief report described the action: "The front line of the enemy soon came within range of our muskets and was repulsed. A portion of their second line succeeded in reaching that part of the works held by the One Hundred and twenty-eighth Indiana, and planted their colors upon them. The color-bearer was killed and the flag fell upon the outside. A number of the enemy succeeded in climbing over the works and were taken prisoners. This charge of the enemy was soon repulsed. . . ."

Probably the fighting described by Stiles is the same presented from the Confederate viewpoint by General Winfield S. Featherston, commander of a brigade in Loring's division, who reported that "the color-bearer of the Thirty-third [Mississippi] was killed some fifteen paces from the works, when Lieutenant H.C. Shaw, of Company K, carried them forward, and when in the act of planting them on the works was killed, his body falling in the trench, the colors falling in the works."

As Stewart's corps was being thrown back on the army's right, elsewhere on the field Hood's attack was also blunted by lack of coordination. On the Confederate left, General Bate, having farther to march than any other division in the army, was not able to bring his command into the first grand charge. Bate's After Action Report describes the route of march in the following words: "About three o'clock . . . I was ordered by General Cheatham to move my command by the left flank, pass a gap in the ridge to the left, circle around a mound which rose in the plain below, and move forward toward the Carter Creek turnpike, until, in a direct advance on the town of Franklin, my left would strike the house of Mrs. Rebecca Bostick. I lost no time in starting and moved rapidly," Bate avowed. "This gave me the arc, while the divisions on my right moved on the chord of the circle."

Even with a rapid march, Bate had so much farther to go that Brown and Cleburne hit the Federal line well before he could get into position to assault. With the repulse of Brown and Cleburne, and the sealing of the breach at the Columbia Pike near the Carter house, the battle's most critical moment, for Confederate and Federal alike, had passed. But the fight was far from being over. Mr. Carter would later recall, and attempt to verbalize, the feelings of those still in the cellar of the house: "The first onset having passed, and no one harmed," he said, "reassurance returned, and hope revived with some; with others, the comparative lull increased the tension and awakened fears of unknown dangers yet to come."

# 6 /

# Hell . . . Exploded in Our Faces

Issac Shannon had watched Hood's army move forward to this first attack. Shannon, a sharpshooter in the Ninth Tennessee Infantry, had spent the early afternoon making life miserable for the artillerymen of Wagner's advance division. The sharpshooter and his comrades occupied the advanced point of Merrill Hill. Shannon's Whitworth gun and telescopic sight proved deadly for the gunners of Company A, Second Missouri Artillery.

Later, after the war, Shannon would learn just how accurate his aim had been against gun position number one. After Appomattox, marksman Shannon resided in the hamlet of Goodlettsville, just north of Nashville. Another resident was the brother of one of the gunners, and furnished the names of the four artillerymen Shannon shot down that afternoon.

Then Shannon's work was interrupted as Cheatham's and Stewart's corps moved forward. The marksman recalled how Cheatham's men swept around Merrill Hill, moving as "a great wave" against Wagner's line. The Federal advance fell back in disorder, and Shannon watched as Cheatham pressed on to the main line of Yankee works. Then fire and smoke erupted and there was nothing more to be seen. "All was obscured by smoke," the rifleman remembered.

No one who was there could forget the fury of that first

assault. J.C. Dean, a member of the Third Mississippi Regiment, lived to remember the murderous fire as Cleburne's men came panting up the Columbia road against the cotton gin and the road opening at the Carter House. A "deadly hail of lead and iron" struck the Confederates, and men "fell at almost every step." Dr. James M'Neilly, a chaplain in Quarles's brigade, kept busy organizing an emergency field hospital near the McGavock home at Carnton. Soon, beaten soldiers from French's division staggered back with tales of the incredible slaughter wrought by Casement's repeating rifles. The storm of bullets had been so intense that men "pulled their hats over their faces, as if to shield them from a storm of hail." Private W.A. Washburn of the First Arkansas Regiment had charged into the fray in Govan's brigade near the Columbia road. He later recalled that the Federal fire from the main line was "a besom of destruction." Even years after the war, Washburn evinced his frustration when the Yankees did not retreat. He remembered how his unit had literally climbed the works only to discover the Union boys would not fall back. "We had never seen the Federals fail to run before under like circumstances," he admitted.

Across the breastworks, a Union soldier of Casement's brigade, Tillman Stevens, had watched Hood's men come up the Columbia road. Stevens had lounged on the gentle slope in front of the Carter family's cotton gin while he lunched. Neither he nor his comrades showed much interest in Hood's men. The Confederates indeed were visible out along Winstead and Breezy hills, in view "just as plainly as we could see our own."

The remainder of the leisurely meal was soon forgotten. Hood's men rolled forward, and officers shouted urgent calls for the troops to stand to arms. Stewart's and Cheatham's men were so visible and awesome in appearance that, years later, the Union veteran said, "It looked to me as though the whole South had come up there and were determined to walk right over us." It was not Dixie, only Cleburne's men who tore into the position held by Stevens and his comrades. "We kept pouring the fire," Stevens said, while the Confederates fell "like leaves in the fall of the year."

★ ★ ★

ALL remembered well that first assault just before sunset, which was a screaming frenzy of smoke, yells, the sickening thud of

[ 125

large-caliber bullets striking another human, and a score of other sounds. Later, when the passions cooled, when the survivors were old men with canes and impressive gray beards, they spoke as much—or more—of the second stage of the carnage at Franklin. Once the gap at the Columbia road had been sealed, the fight became more holocaust than battle.

From dusk until about 9 o'clock that night, when the firing died down, Franklin was actually five different battles. During this time, the Confederate high command knew little of what was happening. Hood remained at his headquarters on the Winstead Hill range, and the accounts available indicate that he knew practically nothing of what was happening to his army. Even in the daylight hours he could not see anything, due to the fierce cloud of smoke covering the ground as soon as the first attack occurred. Darkness came soon on the last day of November, and the early night hours were filled only with incessant flashes of rifle and artillery fire. Frank Cheatham had ridden forward to a rocky eminence on the west side of the Nashville-Columbia pike, so that he could supervise the battle. There is little evidence that even Cheatham understood the slaughter that was occurring, especially since there were few left to report to him. For example, in General John C. Brown's division, every general officer—including the commander—had been killed, wounded, or captured.

The tragedy of Brown's position west of the Columbia road has been recounted many times, although the exact timing of events has been obscured in the bedlam of that afternoon. The fight of Brown's troops west of the road, as mentioned, was one of five uncoordinated assaults Hood's army made once the original attack had faltered.

Ironically, that portion of Brown's line west of the road had been the most successful. The brigades of Generals Strahl, Gist, and Carter had stormed the main Federal works just south of the Carter House with such ferocity that, as a Union veteran remembered, the Confederates "lifted Strickland's front line out of the works by the force of their impact. . . ." The counter-move by Colonel Emerson Opdycke's brigade and other units had forced Brown's men back to the main Federal line. But the Federals never re-occupied this segment of their works to the west of the Columbia road and south of the Carter House.

Instead, a curious, Texas-style battle developed along an

entire brigade front west of the road. Once Brown's men were driven back to the main earthworks, they remained on the outer side of the earthworks until the battle ended. The Federals never regained a position on the north side of their main breastworks in this sector of the line. Instead, they remained behind the retrenchment, or second line of earthworks, which extended from the road westward across the Carter House property, directly south of the office and smokehouse that still stand today. During the twilight hours, a barricade was hastily constructed across the garden of the Carter residence to extend this second line. Four guns of the Sixth Ohio were positioned just west of the Carter smokehouse, where this second line of Federal works bent back to the northwest across the Carter property, to a point near the present-day museum at the rear of the Carter shrine. For hours the enemies fired at one another across the yard and gardens of the Carter home.

Once Brown's men had been forced back to the main Federal works, the battle on this front changed from the movements of orderly units of soldiers into an individual's war. There is little evidence that the men of the brigades of Strahl, Gist, and Carter west of the pike regrouped for any large-scale assaults. There were repeated attacks into the night hours by small, isolated units, but not by the division as a whole. The truth was that Brown's men west of the pike were pinned down in the outer ditch of the main works. Colonel Ellison Capers of Gist's brigade recalled that "torn and exhausted . . . the division had only strength enough left to hold its position."

The task of holding the position meant simply that for the next four hours or more, the survivors in the ditch clambered up the earthworks and fired beyond the Carter house, at an enemy less than two hundred feet away. Dead and wounded were piled up in the ditches in a horrible fashion. The Confederates could not move forward, but they could not retreat either, lest they be shot down once the protective cover of the outer ditch was abandoned.

By the end of the first assault, which had broken the Federal lines initially, Brown's division west of the road had lost control. The reason was obvious. Every general officer was killed or wounded west of the pike. Already in the first assault, the South Carolinian, General States Right Gist, had been shot down. He had moved among his men in the area west of the pike while the Federal line was broken, and waved his hat with encouragement. Gist

moved toward his right, to a point near the Columbia road. A bullet felled his horse, and he contined on foot until he was shot through the chest.

When Brown's first assault, led by Gist and Gordon, had faltered, the reserve brigades of Generals Otho Strahl and John C. Carter were ordered forward. Both generals were soon shot down; evidently they fell in the twilight hour after the initial attack in the Carter House sector had been repulsed. Strahl urged his brigade forward in support of Gist's men, just on the west side of the Columbia Pike. Someone recalled later that Strahl, earlier on the hill slopes, had warned his brigade that the attack would be short and desperate.

When his brigade reached the outer side of the main earthworks, Strahl found himself entrapped along with the others. The incredible fire cut down his men in a frightful way. One soldier who stood near Strahl remembered later that the men stood literally on the bodies of the dead and wounded as they reached to fire over the breastworks, or hand guns up to those on top.

By dusk all semblance of command had vanished. Strahl clung to the ditch like any private soldier. A companion in the ghastly ditch recalled that the general had been handing up an Enfield rifle to a Rebel posted atop the earthworks. The soldier was shot down, and Strahl called for a replacement. The observer scrambled up the earthwork while his brigade commander stood on bodies in the ditch loading weapons. Then General Otho Strahl was shot three times and fell dead.

By nightfall, not long after the failure of the first assault, Brown's division west of the pike was totally out of control. Brown himself was badly wounded near the works during the melee. General John C. Carter had led his brigade forward after the failure of the first assault to reinforce Gist near the Carter House. He was mortally wounded; ten days later Carter died at the Harrison home south of Winstead Hill.

By nightfall, Brown's losses were incredible. The division commander lay wounded. All three brigade leaders who directed affairs west of the Columbia road were dead or dying. In Gist's command, for example, a major remained the senior officer of the brigade by nightfall, since every superior had been killed or wound-

---

General John C. Carter.

ed. By 9 P.M., a captain remained as the senior leader of the entire brigade. Strahl's command suffered no less heavily. Strahl and his entire staff were killed, and three regimental leaders were killed or wounded.

Why did Brown's men west of the pike suffer this high rate of casualties? Two reasons explain the carnage. First, Confederate leadership broke down here. Clearly, Hood and Cheatham, on separate hills south of the town and in the rear of the battle, did not understand the nature of the fight near the Columbia road. There was no leadership in the rear, and due to unbelievable casualties among the unit commanders, there was no direction at the front. Brown's men west of the pike were in effect doomed to remain where they were and fight as individuals, reform in small, defiant bands, or scamper through the locust abatis to the rear.

The slaughter came also because of the condition of affairs to the east and west. East of the Columbia pike, near the present intersection of the pike and Cleburne Avenue, the battle was quite different. For a front of almost two brigades east of the pike, the fight was being made by General George Gordon's brigade of Brown's division and by General Patrick Cleburne's entire division.

Somehow most of Gordon's brigade had veered across the Columbia pike during the original pursuit of Wagner's men and the breakthrough of the main line just below the Carter home. Gordon himself later explained why this had happened and could only blame it on "the rush and confusion." When the frightened infantry of Wagner's command fled pell-mell back through the road gap, past the Carter residence, the pursuers were an intermingled mass of Gordon's outfit, together with elements of Cleburne's left wing, particularly the brigade of General H.B. Granbury.

The attackers on this side of the Columbia road failed to drive the Federals permanently from the main works. In the initial assault, the right wing of General James Reilly's brigade, hard by the Columbia pike, had collapsed in the confusion that followed the frantic retreat of Wagner's men from the advanced position. The Kentucky regiments led by Lieutenant-Colonels Laurence Rosseau and John White had aided in driving the invaders back beyond the Carter House and main line of works.

Here, after the first assault had failed, a peculiar situation was evident. West of the road, three brigades of Brown's division had

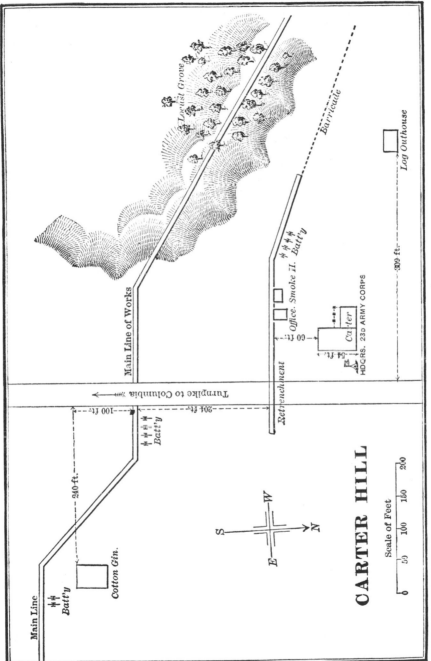

MAP 5. CARTER HILL. *From Jacob D. Cox, The Battle of Franklin.*

succeeded in driving the Union infantry from the main works to a new line at the Carter House. But east of the road, where Cleburne's division and Gordon's brigade had stormed through the breach, the Union forces under Reilly succeeded in regaining the inner side of the main breastworks.

The effect was to cause disaster for General John C. Brown's men just west of the Columbia pike, in front of the Carter House. By twilight, after the first attack had failed, they were subjected to a horrendous crossfire. Strickland's beaten men had rallied in the yard of the Carter House. To the west, more fire came from the units positioned toward the Carter's Creek Pike. But the worst onslaught came from across the Columbia road, in the vicinity of the Carter cotton gin. The brief counterthrust had restored the Federal works on the east side of the Columbia pike, near the present-day intersection of Cleburne Avenue and the pike. The men of Gordon's brigade and Cleburne's division clung to the outer edge of these earthworks after the first repulse and throughout the night.

But the Federal hold on these trenches east of the pike spelled doom for Brown's division on the west side in front of the Carter House. This was due to the peculiar angle in the earthworks from the Carter cotton gin westward to the Columbia pike. The Union soldiers on the right flank of Casement's brigade, and for much of the front of Reilly's brigade, were actually south of Brown's attackers across the Columbia road. In fact, at the point where the Yankee line began to angle back toward the pike, there was a position, almost two hundred feet in length, where the Federals could pour fire into the flank of Brown's men across the road. One soldier, E. Shapard, of Bedford County, Tennessee, was trapped across the pike with Strahl's men. Later he remembered that "the heavy firing by the Federals was not from the rear of the works at the Carter house, but from the east of the pike. . . . The floor of the trench on the outer side of the embankment was so completely covered with our dead and wounded that there was not standing room for the living."

Directly on the east side of the Columbia pike, the situation was just as bad, if not worse. After the first attack had been repulsed, the remnants of General Gordon's brigade of Brown's division and part of Cleburne's command were driven back to the outer ditch of the main earthworks, just south and west of the

Carter cotton gin. Only a few yards away, the Union soldiers of Reilly's and Casement's brigades clung to the inner ditch of the earthworks.

From twilight until the battle ended, it became less of a fight and more of a slaughter on the sector of the earthworks between the cotton gin and the Columbia pike. Gordon's men huddled in the outer ditch along with the remnants of Granbury's brigade and part of Govan's brigade. The Ohio regiments, only a few feet away, had strengthened their earthworks with head-logs, as noted earlier. Now, soldiers of both armies thrust rifles through the opening between the logs and earthworks and fired point-blank. Others grasped the hair or uniform of an enemy and dragged him over the breastworks. General Jacob Cox had positioned a battery of the Sixth Ohio Light Artillery directly in front of the cotton gin, and Cleburne's men repeatedly tried to force their way through an embrasure in the works where one gun was mounted; they were driven back in wild hand-to-hand combat where men swung rifles, axes, picks, and staves.

By nightfall, Gordon's and Cleburne's men were trapped in a horrible crossfire. Remnants of Gordon's brigade jammed into the ditch just east of the road, together with survivors of Granbury's brigade and part of General D.C. Govan's command. During the brief period between the end of the first assault and darkness, some regiments managed to re-form and launch a second assault against the embankments in the vicinity of the cotton gin. When it failed, the remainder of the fight on this sector became little more than a personal struggle for survival.

The enemy lay not only in front of the Rebels but on their right as well. Some 250 feet east of the Columbia pike, the Federal works turned at that deadly angle. The Ohio regiments were able to pour a withering fire at the side and rear of the Confederate line huddled in the outer ditch. By darkness all semblance of command had long since broken down. One Federal officer recalled that Hood's men on this part of the line resembled milling sheep in a pen, as they struggled for protective cover under the fire. Colonel Oscar Sterl of the One Hundred and Fourth Ohio Regiment, after watching the fight from near the cotton gin, remarked that the Union fire was "cutting down by the hundreds rebels who had accumulated and massed in the ditches and immediately in front."

One of Cleburne's soldiers, a private in Govan's brigade,

was trapped in the angle between the turn in the Federal line and the Columbia pike and lived to recall the horror. Private W.A. Washburn wrote later that he and his comrades lay in the ditch, attempting to find cover from the enfilading fire. Meanwhile they were threatened by Yankee rifles thrust through the headlogs above them, and sometimes even threw dirt into the faces of their adversaries. It was a trap, and just east of the road, men fell by the hundreds.

Who could lead them back? Hood's and Cheatham's positions were too distant for them to understand what was happening along the Columbia road. General George Gordon could not lead his men to the rear. By dark, he was a Union prisoner. Later, some writers would describe how Gordon was captured when he led his men through the breach in the entrenchments at the Columbia pike during the first assault.

By accounts of people who were there—including Gordon himself—this is not accurate. Later, General Gordon spoke of the absolute chaos on the field after Wagner's advance division broke and retreated toward the Carter House. More than once, the veteran Confederate officer recounted the moment of his capture. Evidently Gordon was by no means in the front of his brigade—this is apparent from his clear observation of everything done by his men. He recalled how his troops joined in the rout of Wagner's division, pursued them down the Columbia pike, and how he had yelled, "Go into the works with them!"

Some went and were captured, but General Gordon did not get that far. He remembered later that "within a hundred paces of their main line . . . it seemed to me that hell itself had exploded in our faces." Then came "a storm of shot and shell, canister and musketry . . .," and soon "the field was covered at this point with a mantle of dead and dying men." Still Gordon moved forward to the main line of entrenchments. By his own admission, he was not present with his men who, in forlorn hope, pushed through the gap at the Columbia pike. In one post-war reminiscence, Gordon described how his line and those of Granbury's brigade of Cleburne's division became intermingled as they approached the main line of breastworks. Meanwhile the Federals had massed such destructive firepower near the pike that "most of us halted in the ditch on the outside. . . ."

A second post-war account by Gordon confirms that he did not penetrate the main line of earthworks. In this memoir, Gordon recalled that his and Granbury's men had rushed forward amid the hail of fire "until we reached the enemy's works; but being so exhausted and so few in numbers, we halted in the ditch on the outside. . . ."

So General Gordon and his men had rushed into a trap, unable to push across the earthworks and afraid to retreat. Today a visitor to the Franklin field can stand at the present intersection of the Columbia pike and Cleburne Avenue and envision Gordon's dilemma a few hundred feet to the east, and over a century ago. Gordon and the other survivors of his brigade clung to the outer ditch of the parapet south of the Garter cotton gin. He watched during the hour before sunset as a few men tried to scramble across the earthworks but were "clubbed to the earth with musketry or pierced with bayonets." Like the others in the ditch, Gordon engaged in a random fire against Reilly's men on the opposite side. The Confederates would reach upward with a single arm and thrust a weapon through the slit beneath the head-logs in order to fire.

Thus some of Franklin's greatest carnage took place here, in the 240-foot sector of the ditch between the Columbia pike and the sharp angle in the Federal line, as Confederates in the angle—Gordon's men and part of Granbury's command—were subjected to a murderous crossfire from three directions. On the east, they not only received the infantry fire of Reilly's and Casement's men at the angle of the line but were also hit by artillery barrages from across the Harpeth River. Reilly's men fired point-blank across the ditch on their front. Meanwhile, the Confederates were enfiladed by infantry fire from their left from the back grounds of the Carter family property.

No body of infantry could withstand such punishment. In the last minutes before dusk, the Confederates in the angle began to surrender. Hats or caps were placed on bayonets, and men shouted "cease firing!" Groups surrendered at a time, although Gordon at first would not budge. He remained on a portion of the line manned by one other Confederate soldier, and suggested that if the two survivors endured until darkness, they could crawl among the bodies of the killed and wounded and reach the rear.

Finally Gordon himself gave up, remarking that the two

men would be killed if they remained in the ditch. He handed a handkerchief to his comrade, who hoisted it and began climbing the works. A beaten General George Gordon followed.

Just to the east, the remainder of Cheatham's corps was being slaughtered. In the attack, Cleburne had shifted his lines to a two-brigade front, with Granbury's on the west near the Columbia pike and General D.C. Govan's on the right, with General Mark Lowrey's brigade as a reserve. In terms of location, Cleburne's position covered roughly the center of the Federal line entrenched between the Carter's Creek and Lewisburg pikes. His three brigades contested the entire front of General James Reilly's brigade and part of the length of the fortifications defended by General John S. Casement's brigade. In other words, Cleburne's section of the line covered approximately 30 percent of the Union fortifications between the Columbia and Lewisburg pikes.

The fate of Cleburne's three brigades at Franklin was nothing short of a slaughter. As mentioned previously, part of his left brigade—General Hiram Granbury's—broke through at the Columbia pike gap or became trapped in the angle of Federal breastworks just east of the pike. After the first repulse, the remnants of Granbury's men mingled with Govan's brigade on the south side of the earthworks. Even after dark, supported by General Mark Lowrey's brigade, these men engaged in what General J.S. Casement described as "several distinct charges," which were repulsed "with great slaughter." General James Reilly remembered that Cleburne's troops made "various and continual assaults," which "were each time repulsed with fearful slaughter."

Later, the cold statistics would record the horror experienced by Cleburne's men that evening. Fourteen of Cleburne's brigade and regimental commanders were listed as killed, wounded, or missing. Losses were heavy on all brigade fronts. Even before the first breakthrough in the line had been repulsed, General Hiram Granbury had been shot through the head while urging his men onward near the Columbia pike. Five other regimental leaders were killed or listed as missing.

Eastward along Cleburne's line, the same dismal situation existed between the repulse of the first attack and the battle's end later that night. Govan's brigade marched into a hailstorm of repeating-rifle fire from Casement's brigade. From about 5 P.M., when the first assault was repulsed, until 9 P.M., when the battle began to ebb, conditions on Govan's front were no better. Some of his troops clung to the outer works of the Federal line, afraid to retreat lest they be shot down. Others fell back, reinforced by General Mark Lowrey's brigade, to make repeated, bullish assaults in which some men climbed the earthworks only to be shot down or taken prisoner.

For about four hours, from approaching darkness until the battle began to cease, there was little command direction on Cleburne's front. The battle became more an individual soldier's fight to survive. Govan and Lowrey suffered intense officer losses, and there was little direction to be given. For example, Lowrey carried five regiments into the fight, mostly Mississippi and Alabama troops. Four of the colonels leading his regiments were casualties, while a fifth lieutenant-colonel was wounded. Govan lost three regimental leaders. Later, after the war, Lowrey recalled watching while what he estimated as one-half of his men were shot down attempting to storm the works defended by Reilly and Casement. Lowrey rode to within thirty feet of the earthworks and decided he could do little more than go to the rear and gather up the fragments of the division.

No matter how many men Lowrey could have gathered, the division would never be the same. General Patrick Cleburne, one of the finest leaders the South possessed in 1864, had been shot down during the melee of the first assault. Back on Winstead Hill, before the army moved forward with the regimental flags, bands, and other trappings of a dying kind of war, Cleburne had been in a despondent mood.

Ruffled and hurt, he stood with his brigade leader and friend, General D.C. Govan, on the Winstead Hill slope. Already a mood of Celtic fatalism seemed to overcome the general. Earlier he had ridden out to Merrill Hill to view the Yankee lines through the sharpshooter's telescopic sight, as mentioned earlier. On that trek, he swept the field with the scope and murmured, "They have three lines of works." Cleburne looked again and then added, "And they are all completed." He rode back to Winstead Hill where Govan and the others waited for the attack. The Arkansan Govan saluted and bade Cleburne goodbye, remarking that few of them would get back to Arkansas. Cleburne replied, "Well, Govan, if we are to die, let us die like men." Soon Cleburne rode forward for the last time.

Patrick Ronayne Cleburne, known by many as "the Stonewall Jackson of the West," would die a long way from his birthplace in Ovens Township, County Cork, Ireland. Bridepark Cottage, where he was born, remains today, together with other landmarks of the family. There is St. Mary's Church in the Parish of Anthnowen where Cleburne was baptized. His father, Dr. Joseph Cleburne, is buried there.

The family's fortunes had seen hard times after Dr. Cleburne's death. Young Patrick, scarcely fifteen, was chosen by his family to become a doctor like his father. But in 1846 Pat Cleburne failed the entrance examination at the Dublin medical school. Cleburne feared that he had disgraced the family name. He ran away to join the British army, rising by 1849 to the rank of corporal. Cleburne's family, meanwhile, seeking a better life, decided that same year to move to America. Young Patrick Cleburne purchased his army discharge and joined in the Great Adventure.

Home in the New World eventually became Helena, Arkansas. In the decade before the Civil War, Cleburne rose rapidly in local society as a druggist and later an attorney who was active in politics. The advent of the war saw the same steady, determined drive for excellence. As first a brigade and later a division commander, Cleburne's splendid record became part of the history of Shiloh, Perryville, Murfreesboro, Chickamauga, and every other major western battle.

Yet, curiously, Cleburne—although twice voted the gratitude of the Confederate Congress—watched as others were advanced beyond him to the rank of corps commander. Men such as Stewart and Stephen Lee, of less known ability, rose to outrank him—a strong case that political factors within the Army of Tennessee held back Cleburne's promotion. Cleburne, always close to his friend and long-time corps leader General William Hardee, had been a critic of General Braxton Bragg. Bragg commanded the army from the early summer of 1862 until the end of 1863—the longest tenure of service for any leader of the strife-ridden Army of Tennessee during the war. Hardee and Bragg became sworn enemies, and Cleburne had joined others in 1863 to advocate openly Bragg's removal from command after the battle of Chickamauga. Later in 1864, after General Joseph Johnston assumed army command, Cleburne gained other enemies by proposing in a famous meeting at army headquarters in Georgia that slaves be emancipated if they would fight for the Confederacy. This, too, no doubt dampened his chances for promotion.

Perhaps frustration over lack of promotion welled up in Cleburne on that Indian summer afternoon. Maybe the burning hurt over the Spring Hill matter drove the proud, sensitive officer to prove something. It perhaps went even deeper, back into his Celtic soul, back to his ancestor who had fought at Tewksbury and Bosworth centuries earlier. *Something* drove on Patrick Cleburne that day, down Winstead Hill, past Merrill Hill's eminence, and onward to the Federal earthworks. He came to the Union lines in the manner of a private, not a division commander.

General George Gordon never forgot the sight. Years later, Gordon could remember the scene. Wagner's advance line had been broken. Gordon and his men were racing along the Columbia pike toward the gap in the line. Suddenly Cleburne appeared on horseback, racing his mount in diagonal fashion through his own division and toward the enemy earthworks. Gordon was forced to halt quickly lest Cleburne's horse "trampled me to the earth." Then Cleburne passed out of Gordon's sight.

Now General D.C. Govan, Cleburne's close friend and brigade leader, watched as his commander neared the Federal works. Cleburne's horse was wounded by a Federal artillery piece posted near the Carter cotton gin. One of Cleburne's aides dismounted and offered his mount. Cleburne was in the act of mounting the animal when a second cannonball killed the horse. Govan watched as Cleburne moved forward on foot. The Irishman then walked toward the Federal works, waving his cap. Cleburne disappeared into the battle smoke. Govan recalled that it was the last time he saw Cleburne alive.

The heavy losses in the Confederate center experienced by Brown's and Cleburne's divisions were due in part to a lack of coordination on both the left and the right. On the left, the attack was made by General William Bate's division. Bate was a natural leader with a colorful past who had experienced a rapid rise to command in the war. A native of the Middle Tennessee bluegrass, Bate had quit school to work on a Mississippi River steamboat and then had served as a private in the Mexican War. After a subsequent career in law and politics, Bate joined the Confederate service as a mere private. By the end of 1861 he had been promoted to colonel of the Second Tennessee Regiment. Shortly before the battle of Perryville in 1862, Bate became a brigadier-general, and by early 1864 he was a major-general of his own division. After the war he served two terms as governor of Tennessee and four as United States senator.

He, too, was one of the last. Back in 1863, it had been part of Bate's division that contested General William S. Rosecrans at the battle of Hoover's Gap, which opened the door to an advance on Chattanooga. Bate's command, by some accounts, fired the first gun near Thedford's Ford on Chickamauga Creek later in September. Bate's troops chewed sorghum stalks as they waited for the bloody Chickamauga battle, and then moved forward for two days' hard fighting that saw the General lose two horses in combat. Bate later was praised for gallantry in the battle along Missionary Ridge, battled Sherman's bluecoats at Resaca and at Atlanta, and afterward had come to Franklin.

Now the veteran officer approached one of his most difficult assignments. General John Hood, from his perch on Winstead Hill, had not understood the situation on the Federal right wing between the Carter's Creek Pike and the river. In fact, one wonders if Hood even knew that Schofield's line extended beyond the pike. About three o'clock that afternoon, Bate was ordered to assume responsibility for the extreme left wing of Cheatham's corps's infantry assault.

A reading of Bate's report of the battle and reference to a topographic map of the area explain much of the Confederate debacle at Franklin. Bate was ordered to form his division with *his left brigade,* that of General Thomas Benton Smith, along the east side of the Carter's Creek Pike. General Henry Jackson's brigade would move on the right, while General Jesse Finley's brigade, under the command of Colonel Robert Bullock, would form a reserve. Bate was instructed to move on the Franklin works with his extreme left regiment guided by the location of the house of Mrs. Rebecca Bostick. The Widow Bostick's house was in a hollow, almost directly south of the point where the Louisville and Nashville Railroad crosses the Carter's Creek Pike today, and it was almost due west of General George Wagner's advanced position on the Columbia pike, just south of the same railroad.

Bate's orders indicate one of two things about Hood's perception of Schofield's line, both of which were equally disastrous. First, Hood—frustrated by many things—may have been obsessed with smashing Schofield's center and driving the enemy into the river. There is strong evidence of that from those who spoke with him that early afternoon on Winstead Hill. Bate on the far left had no reinforcement except the solitary cavalry division commanded by General James Chalmers. Second, Hood simply may have been ignorant of the presence of Schofield's line west of the Carter's Creek Pike. Evidently, Bate himself was surprised to find Union soldiers west of the road. Regardless of the answer, Hood lost a splendid opportunity to bypass Schofield's strong earthworks in the center and left of the Federal line.

There was another serious problem. Hood's attack plans for Cheatham and Stewart gave Bate no leeway for the length of time required to make the lengthy march. Bate's men stepped off with the rest of the attacking force but were required to march a far greater distance. Due to the nature of the hilly terrain on his front, Bate could not move forward directly. Instead, he marched the division through a gap in the slopes between the modern-day Williamson Memorial Gardens and Winstead Hill, north of Polk Creek, until he struck the Carter's Creek Pike. This circuitous path forced Bate's men to move over a mile almost at right angles to the main attacking force to reach the vicinity of the Carter's Creek Pike. Bate's command then wheeled westward around the large dome near the road, almost 1,000 feet high, which is occupied today by a radio tower just east of the pike. Now, at last, Bate thought, he could attack the enemy.

It was not that simple. Hood's original attack plan had not called for Bate's left brigade, that of General Thomas Benton Smith *to even* reach the Carter's Creek Pike. Hood's plan was for Smith's brigade to be positioned relatively far east of the pike, aligning on the home of Mrs. Rebecca Bostick.

A combination of timing, Hood's poor reconnaissance, and the terrain combined to turn the attack by Bate's division and Chalmers's dismounted cavalry division into a series of uncoordinated assaults by various brigades. On Bate's right, Jackson's brigade swept east of the Bostick house and joined in the rout of Wagner's hapless men in the advanced position. Jackson's men rushed onward to the main Federal works and attacked just to the left of General John C. Brown's division. Like Brown's men, Jackson's troops moved across open ground to the works on the rear of the Carter farm. They were hit with massive fire from Colonel Orlando Moore's brigade. Jackson's brigade was unable to break Moore's line as Brown had done to Strickland's brigade to the east in front of the Carter House. They drew back, probably about 4:30 P.M., to re-form for another assault.

Evidently the first assault had come more slowly in Bate's center. While approaching the Bostick house in the original march, Bate discovered an advanced Union skirmish line posted near the house. This was enough to tell Bate that Schofield's line was longer than he had assumed. So there was a pause while the left of Smith's brigade changed direction and extended the line all the way to the Carter's Creek Pike.

Even this did not prove to be enough. As Smith's brigade pushed onward past the Bostick house toward the main line of works, the Confederates were met with what Bate described as a "furious fire" from Union riflemen west of the Carter's Creek Pike. Bate was understandably frustrated, as is evidenced by the wording of his official report. The presence of Union troops in strength across the pike was a surprise. Also, Bate had assumed that his infantry flank would be protected by the dismounted cavalry of General James Chalmers's division. Chalmers's men were supposed to advance on Bate's left, west of the Carter's Creek pike. Yet when the attack rolled forward, Chalmers had lagged behind and not extended his line eastward to join Bate.

Even while Jackson's brigade was assaulting the works, Bate was forced to delay the attack on the left to adjust for the unexpected development. Bate had only one reserve—Finley's Florida brigade. Now it was moved onto the main line, extending the position west across the pike.

From the initial repulse of Jackson's brigade on the right until the battle ended that night, the story of Bate's division was one of disconcerted attacks and lost opportunities. Jackson's initial repulse had come not long after 4 P.M. According to the Union commander, General William Grose, Finley's Florida brigade did not even reach his works until almost one hour later. Jackson through the evening re-formed his lines and made repeated strikes against the earthworks, as did General Thomas Benton Smith's brigade in the center. They had no support during this furious struggle of almost five hours, when some Confederates leaped atop the works to plant flags, only to be shot down.

On the left, Finley's brigade possessed two regiments in the sector west of the Carter's Creek Pike. They attacked bravely but were too weak to threaten even the hastily dug Federal entrenchments in front of General William Grose's men. The first assault came about 5 P.M., in an attack about which Grose commented, "The destruction to the enemy was terrible." Few of Finley's Confederates got within one hundred yards of the Federal line. They withdrew to the vicinity of the Bostick house, re-formed lines, and charged again in the growing darkness, some one-half hour later, only to be repulsed again.

On Hood's far left, Chalmers's division had done little to help Bate. In all fairness, it was more a "division" in name than actuality, since Chalmers carried only one full brigade and another single regiment into the battle. Still, Chalmers's men did perform badly in the battle on the far Confederate left, against the Union brigades of Generals I.M. Kirby and Walter C. Whitaker. Kirby's midwestern regiments were the first ones engaged by Chalmers. They held the center of the arc between the Carter's Creek Pike and the river. So weak was the Confederate assault that it was repulsed after the Federals fired "two or three volleys," and Kirby even advanced skirmishers to hold permanent positions until the battle ended. On the far right, General Walter Whitaker's troops met even less of a challenge. According to Whitaker, Chalmers's men fought only about fifteen minutes "when they broke and fled, to return no more. . . ." Chalmers admitted later that his men never reached the Federal line, but that only the Confederate skirmishers advanced within sixty yards of the Union position. Here Chalmers reported that "my force was too small to justify an attempt to storm" the Yankee lines, and decided merely to "only hold my position." Chalmers's casualty figures tell the story of his feeble struggle. During the entire month of November, including the Spring Hill affair, Chalmers's total loss in killed and wounded was an aggregate of fifty-six men. Off to the east that afternoon at Franklin, another Confederate division, that of Cleburne, lost over 1,700 men.

★ ★ ★

THE same lack of a concerted effort that doomed Bate's hopes also plagued Stewart's corps on the right wing. Prior to the repulse of the first assault shortly after 4 P.M., nothing had gone well for "Old Straight" Stewart. Like Bate, A.P. Stewart was one of the very last leaders who had been with the Army of Tennessee in years which had been more kind. In the early summer of 1861, Stewart was the first Confederate leader to occupy Island Number 10 and New Madrid, Missouri. Stewart fought Grant at the battle of Belmont, Missouri, and then led a brigade in Polk's corps through the carnage of Shiloh, Perryville, and Murfreesboro. "Old Straight" led a division in the battles of Chickamauga and Chattanooga and then followed with General Joe Johnston in the long retreat line to Atlanta through northern Georgia. Finally, Stewart took command of the corps after General Leonidas Polk was killed at Pine Mountain.

Now A.P. Stewart rode forward in the last great Confederate effort on the western front. Stewart on that Indian summer day was what he had been always, a paradoxical figure as are perhaps most Southerners. He was the quiet, modest man of scholarly bent, once a mathematics professor at West Point and later a professor at Cumberland University in nearby Lebanon, Tennessee. He was also a man of resolve and bravery. At Chickamauga, Stewart had been wounded. He had three horses shot from under him at Resaca. In the battles around Atlanta, he was shot in the middle of the forehead.

How Stewart's heart must have sickened as he watched the last great effort of his corps turn into such a debacle! The first assault had been a disaster. General Samuel G. French's division had reached the works before the attackers on Stewart's center and right, Walthall's and Loring's divisions, could reach the breastworks and had been repulsed before help arrived. In the center, Walthall's division had become disorganized when passing through a thicket of Osage orange bushes and was then torn apart by General John Casement's repeating rifles on that sector of the Union line east of the Carter cotton gin. And on the right, near the Lewisburg pike, General W.W. "Blizzards" Loring had encountered every conceivable obstacle. The presence of the railroad cut near the latter-day Willow Plunge Swimming Pool, just off the Lewisburg Pike, had forced his right brigades to change direction, subjecting them to an unmerciful fire from the Union artillery batteries across the Harpeth River. Meanwhile, Loring's men also had to pick their way through the thick Osage orange hedge, only to find that the main Federal works were protected by an abatis of sharpened sticks that was almost impossible to penetrate.

By the end of the first assault, about 5 P.M., Stewart's effort on the right had degenerated into the same complex of isolated attacks that colored other Confederate efforts that evening. French's division had been torn to bits in the first assault, which had been countered by Casement's repeating rifles. One brigade leader, General Francis M. Cockrell, was wounded, and four other regimental leaders were shot down, killed, or wounded. French's attack broke apart into isolated assaults during the dusk and night hours. Some regimental groups clung to the outer ditch below the Union earthworks while others made repeated, bullish attacks that netted little save more casualties. By the end of the firing that night, French had lost almost 30 percent of his command.

Losses were even worse in the divisions led by Walthall and Loring. At least French's men did have one advantage—they could reach the outer ditch of the Federal works quickly and huddle there until darkness fell. In the center, Walthall's men had enjoyed no such advantage in the first assault or thereafter. Slow progress had been made through the thick Osage orange hedge while Casement's repeating rifles drew dead aim and artillery pounded unmercifully from across the Harpeth River. Besides, there was nothing to shield Walthall's men from the awesome fire. The ground was open totally in his front except for the hedge and the deadly abatis encountered near the main works.

The abatis had provided the *coup de grace* to any united effort in Walthall's first attack. Here and there, companies of men had picked their way through the morass to join the men of Cleburne and French in the ditch beneath the works. Others could venture no closer but fired from beyond the abatis. In either case, the casualties for the next few hours were frightful.

Casualties in the first assault at 4 P.M. had been heavy in particular among the men of General William A. Quarles's brigade. In the initial move on Schofield's main works, Walthall's left brigade, that of General Daniel H. Reynolds, had become entangled in the Osage orange shrubs while Quarles's men rushed on alone to the main earthworks. Here they had been caught among the artillery fire on the right, Casement's repeating rifles on the front, and flanking fire from more repeating guns on the left.

The casualty reports told the story. Quarles was wounded in the head during the first assault; meanwhile his entire staff was killed. Every single regimental commander was shot down. By 9 P.M. that evening, the ranking officer in the brigade was a captain.

On Stewart's right, the saga of General W.W. Loring was the same. Nothing had gone well for Loring that afternoon. Shortly after 4 P.M., after the first line of attack moved forward, some units of Loring's and Walthall's commands had become intermingled because of the obstacles presented by the railroad cut and the Osage orange obstruction. Loring was in a foul mood and rode to discuss the matter with Walthall, who was in a small ravine near the McGavock house. Chaplain James M'Neilly of Quarles's brigade was the sole observer of the conversation. Loring rode up excitedly, berating Walthall for allowing his men to become mixed with the right wing. A lively interchange followed, according to M'Neilly. Then a disgusted Walthall responded, "General Loring, this is no time for a personal quarrel. When the battle is over, you will know where to find me."

Loring's bad moments had only begun. The first assault had shattered his command. His brigades, separated by the Osage orange hedge, bedeviled by the rail cut, and confronted by the abatis, had dissolved into singular bands of desperate men. Casement's repeating rifles cut them to pieces on the front, while artillery swept their ranks at close range from across the river.

After the first attack failed, roughly about 5 P.M., the next four hours were a nightmare for Loring's command. Some units had worked through the abatis to cling to the outer side of the earthworks; others lay behind the abatis and dodged the awful fire. At one point during the first attack, an entire brigade faltered when it encountered the heavy fire and the abatis and began to fall back. An eyewitness recorded Loring's reaction.

Loring rode to the front amid a hail of bullets raining through the abatis. He tried to hold the frightened brigade in place as they fell back. Loring shouted for them to stand fast. Once he cried out in anguish, "Great God: Do I command cowards?" Then Loring turned alone on the horse and faced the enemy fire for over a minute. He was in full Confederate uniform. A sword belt encompassed his waist; sword and scabbard were polished and shone brightly. A large, dark plume of ostrich feathers drooped over his hat. Loring was a perfect target for some Union sharpshooter who had dreamed of felling a Rebel general. He stood alone, however, in one last defiant act by the Army of Tennessee. Then Loring turned and galloped to the rear to re-group the unit.

They were not cowards at all, only humans caught amid a

near massacre. After the first repulse, Loring's brigades were totally broken up into tiny units. Some men in the ditch fought their way across, only to be captured or killed. A second contingent huddled in the outer ditch for hours. Other comrades remained pinned beyond the abatis.

There was no order on Hood's right, only frightful casualties. For example, General John Adams had moved his brigade forward along Loring's right near the Lewisburg road, through the grounds occupied today by the Confederate cemetery. The curvature of the Harpeth River and the railroad cut had forced Adams's men to veer sharply to the west.

Later, a soldier in the Fifteenth Mississippi Regiment recalled the awful punishment endured by Adams's brigade in the wheel to the left. Captain John Bolt recalled how the regimental bands played "Annie Laurie" and "Ben Bolt" as Adams's regiments surged forward under terrific fire. By the time Adams's men had penetrated beyond the abatis in small groups, the acrid gunpowder smoke lay so heavily that "a man could not see ten feet in front of himself." Here the curve in the Harpeth River had so shortened the Confederate front that all semblance of order vanished even during the first assault on Stewart's front. In fact, the lines became so entangled that part of Adams's brigade—including the general himself—found itself not on the far right but on Stewart's far left, adjacent to Cleburne's division.

Here General John Adams fell in the first assault. A Union soldier of Casement's brigade, Tillman Stevens, watched Adams and his men approach the outer works. At first the young general was riding back and forth along the rear of his line, urging his men forward. Perhaps the brigade faltered amid the incredible onslaught of Casement's repeating rifles. For whatever reason, General Adams urged his bay horse to the front of the brigade, spurred his horse, and rode headlong toward the works. Another Union soldier, James Barr of the Sixty-fifth Illinois Volunteers, watched as Adams crossed the ditch and rode his horse onto the parapet. Colonel W. Scott Stewart of the Sixty-fifth Illinois shouted for his men to hold their fire in the face of such a courageous act, and a Union soldier who watched Adams ride astride the works remembered, "We hoped he would not be killed. He was too brave to be killed."

It was too late. Adams reached down and attempted to seize

the regimental flag from the color guard. He was shot down instantly and fell backward into the ditch. The horse was killed and remained through the night with its legs straddling the parapet in a grotesque fashion.

By then darkness had begun to fall. The next few hours on Hood's right wing were little different from matters on other fronts. Individual bands of Confederates—companies, regiments, and other groups—huddled in the outer ditch of Schofield's breastworks amid a continued fire. Officer casualties in Cheatham's and Stewart's corps had been so heavy that little direction could be given on the front lines. By the end of the battle that night, fifty-four regimental leaders had been killed, wounded, or captured.

The tormented John Bell Hood knew little of this as he waited on the Winstead Hill range slopes. Smoke and darkness, combined with distance, robbed him of any view of the situation. A definite lack of communication among the officer corps did the same. In part this was due to heavy command losses. The bad blood over the fiasco at Spring Hill also may have been responsible. Little communication was evident between Hood and Frank Cheatham, whose field headquarters was on Merrill Hill, a mile northward toward Franklin. This was apparent in the curious circumstances surrounding General Stephen Dill Lee's appearance on the field.

Actually General Stephen Lee's advance division, commanded by General Edward Johnson, arrived in the Winstead Hill sector just as the battle was beginning. Lee recalled he arrived near Franklin about 4 P.M., at a time when Hood "was just about attacking the enemy with Stewart's and Cheatham's corps. . . ." Why Hood could not have delayed the attack until Johnson went into position and the second division, General Henry D. Clayton's, came up can be explained only by the general's confused, angry thinking that afternoon.

Once on the field, Lee's men were ill-used due to more shoddy command direction. Lee was ordered to form Johnson's division to the left of the pike behind Cheatham's corps. Then Clayton would be brought forward "in position to support the attack." Although Clayton reported he reached the battle area "late in the afternoon," his division was not used. Clayton was put in

---

General John Adams.

position to attack, "but night mercifully interposed to save us from the terrible scourge which our brave companions had suffered."

General Edward Johnson's three brigades were not so fortunate. Hood's fuzzy instructions to Lee coupled with the terrain and darkness prevented their effective use. Evidently Hood and Cheatham were not communicating well. According to Lee, Hood, "finding that the battle was stubborn . . . ," ordered Lee to go forward "in person to communicate with General Cheatham" and, if necessary, to put Johnson into the battle. Why Hood did not merely dispatch a staff officer at full gallop to confer with Cheatham is curious. Instead, Lee, who knew little of the terrain, was forced to go and find his fellow corps leader. Finally he met Cheatham "about dark" and learned that assistance was needed "at once." It is equally puzzling why Cheatham had not already dispatched his own aide to Hood's headquarters with this news. There are only two possible explanations and perhaps both were responsible. Certainly tension existed between Hood and Cheatham over the Spring Hill matter. Also, Cheatham's officer losses were so heavy and the fighting so confused that he may have known little of the slaughter occurring on his front.

Johnson's men suffered due to this curious situation. Lee now ordered Johnson to move forward. A better word would be "grope" forward. Johnson knew nothing of the terrain, had no evident orders to reinforce a particular point, and groped through the darkness and smoke to Bate's position near the Bostick house. It was about one hour after dark when Johnson struck the Federal works east of the Carter's Creek road. For over two hours, until about 9 P.M., his four brigades attacked repeatedly, in a hard fight with much hand-to-hand combat. General Jacob H. Sharp's brigade made a temporary breach and captured three stands of enemy colors. General William Brantley's Mississippi brigade joined General Zachariah C. Deas's Alabama troops in the hard night fight across the ditch and atop the works held by General Orlando Moore's Federals.

Some of the hardest punishment was taken by General Arthur M. Manigault's South Carolina brigade. The forty-year-old Manigault, a highly intelligent businessman and rice planter, had served the Confederacy from the beginning. He was on Beauregard's staff during Fort Sumter's bombardment in 1861 and later that year commanded a military district in South Carolina under the supervision of departmental leader General Robert E. Lee. The year 1862 took Manigault to the western front, to Perryville and Murfreesboro. After the fight on Stone's River, Manigault was elevated to brigade commander and served well at Chickamauga, Chattanooga, and the long campaign for Atlanta.

After all of that, now Manigault was shot down, severely wounded, in the trenches at Franklin, only months before the war's end. Later in 1886, he would die from the effects of the Franklin wound. Meanwhile, on the cold field that night, Manigault's successor to command the brigade, Colonel Thomas Shaw was killed. His replacement, Colonel Newton Davis, was wounded.

Manigault and the others of Edward Johnson's division led the last formal assault against Schofield's entrenchments. By 9 P.M., the firing had begun to die down, although occasional flashes of rifle or artillery fire lasted for almost two hours. Then the exhausted soldiers of both armies could fight no more.

# 7 /

# The Death of an

# Army

G ENERAL JOHN SCHOFIELD had no intention of resuming the
battle on December 1. Even before Hood's first attack on
November 30, Schofield's intentions were clear. About 3 P.M. he
had received a telegram from General George Thomas in Nashville.
Could Schofield hold the Confederates at Franklin for three days?
Thomas, frantically drawing in reinforcements from St. Louis,
Chattanooga, and elsewhere, needed time to organize his army.

Schofield, fearful of a flanking maneuver, did not think it
could be done and recommended that he fall back to the Brentwood
hills closer to Nashville. At 3:30 Thomas telegraphed his consent to
the evacuation of Franklin. Thirty minutes later, Hood attacked.

About 11 P.M. that night, after the general firing had died
out, Schofield sent orders to his field commanders. The Twenty-
third and Fourth corps would leave the trenches quietly at midnight
and march to the Harpeth River crossings. General Thomas J.
Wood's division would remain at Franklin as a rearguard until all
other units had crossed the river. Then Wood's men would fire the
bridges and join the retreat.

Schofield clearly wanted no more dealings with Hood. He
believed that to remain at Franklin "was to seriously hazard the loss
of my army, by giving the enemy another chance to cut me off from
re-enforcements." Besides, the massive firepower rained on

Hood's army had seriously drained Schofield's ordnance supplies, and he feared there was not enough ammunition available for another hard fight.

But Schofield's worst fear was that he might be out flanked and his communications with Nashville severed. The flanking maneuver by Hood at Spring Hill clearly had intimidated Schofield. This was particularly true in regard to Forrest's rough treatment of General James Wilson's cavalry on November 29. Schofield admitted, "My experience on the 29th had shown how utterly inferior in force my cavalry was to that of the enemy. . . ." On the night of November 30, Schofield believed his "immediate flank and rear were insecure" and that Forrest's presence meant "my communication with Nashville was entirely without protection."

Schofield's remarks concerning the vast numerical superiority of Forrest's cavalry were highly exaggerated. General James Wilson, commander of the army's horsemen, also was prone to offer inflated figures. In his report of the Tennessee campaign, Wilson placed his strength prior to the Spring Hill engagement at 4,300 troopers, and Forrest's strength at "not less than 10,000 men." Forrest's numbers were far less than this. Jackson's division prior to Spring Hill listed 2,001 effectives, which included detached regiments of General George Dibrell's brigade. Forrest's other two divisions, Chalmers's and Buford's, totaled only 3,000 men. Wilson's problem at Spring Hill was not that he was outnumbered—he was outfought.

Wilson also later admitted that he possessed the numerical advantage during the cavalry fight at Franklin. Hood's alignment of his troopers frustrated any efforts by Forrest to push Wilson aside and seize the Nashville road. Chalmers's division—the largest cavalry force—was taken away from Forrest and sent to the far left flank beyond Cheatham's corps. In like manner, Buford's division was dismounted and ordered to join the infantry attack, advancing on the right of Stewart's corps, in the space between the Lewisburg Pike and the Harpeth River. This left only "Red" Jackson's division for any flanking maneuver.

Still, Forrest and Jackson did enough to frighten Schofield and to demonstrate the lost opportunities the Confederates possessed northeast of the Harpeth River. Forrest, with Jackson's division, moved eastward on Henpeck Lane, just south of the Winstead-Breezy Hill range, and reached the Lewisburg Pike. Jackson's men waded the river at Hughes's Ford, some three miles south of Franklin and almost due east of Hood's position on Winstead Hill.

East of the Harpeth, a separate, furious battle raged until after dark. Forrest intended for Jackson's division to move north against the Federal gun positions, which were sweeping Stewart's lines from the sector northeast of the Confederate cemetery. Jackson's men became involved in a heavy fire-fight with Wilson's cavalry on the high ground near McGavock Ford, a crossing of the Harpeth almost due east of the Carnton mansion and Confederate cemetery. Meanwhile, Buford's dismounted cavalry, moving on Stewart's right, had smashed into General John Croxton's cavalry brigade posted along the west side of the river. Buford's men drove the bluecoats across the river at McGavock's ford and then waded the cold waters to join ranks with the men of "Red" Jackson's division. Still, the combined gray force was not strong enough to push back Wilson's troopers and the infantry reinforcements that had been sent from General Thomas Wood's division of the Fourth Corps. Forrest's men were outnumbered at least two-to-one and were short on ammunition. Finally, shortly after 7 P.M., Forrest's troopers fell back across the Harpeth River.

But the display of Rebel power on the Union left only urged General Schofield on in the haste to abandon Franklin. The movement began at midnight. General Jacob Cox went first. His own division, together with Colonel Emerson Opdycke's brigade, left a strong body of skirmishers in the trenches to deceive Hood's men. Then Cox led the column down modern-day Columbia Avenue, past the courthouse square, to a makeshift bridge that had been constructed near the location of the present-day U.S. Highway 31 bridge on the pike to Brentwood and Nashville. Meanwhile, Ruger's division withdrew quietly from the trenches between the Columbia and Carter's Creek pikes, leaving behind a facade of skirmishers. Ruger's brigades moved through the eastern portion of the downtown section of modern-day Franklin.

They crossed the Harpeth River near the present-day intersection of First Avenue and Margin Street. Earlier in the day, soldiers had pulled down fences and ripped boards from adjacent houses. A crude, makeshift bridge of planking was laid across the rails of the Nashville and Decatur Railroad—where the modern-day Louisville and Nashville bridge spans the Harpeth.

The two divisions of Stanley's Fourth Corps, also set for a

retreat at midnight, encountered some difficulty in the withdrawal. They were delayed when mysterious fires broke out in Franklin. The extent of the fires is difficult to ascertain. Later General David Stanley reported that a single house had been set afire and that he suspected Confederate sympathizers had done so to light up the area in the event of a Union retreat. Of course, Stanley by then had been wounded seriously in the throat and was not on the scene. A more careful observer was Lieutenant-Colonel Joseph Fullerton, Stanley's chief of staff. Fullerton kept a long and precise journal of the campaign and recorded in meticulous fashion the time of every event. Fullerton reported that the fires involved more than one building and "lighted the country for miles around." Meanwhile, Stanley's aides located an old fire engine in Franklin and extinguished the flames. Actually, the heavy cover of smoke only aided Schofield in his covert withdrawal.

About 12:30 A.M. Kimball's and Wagner's divisions marched quietly through the town and joined the Twenty-third Corps on the north bank of the Harpeth River. At 2 A.M. the men of the picket line began to fall back from the main fortifications and join their comrades north of the river. Shortly before 3 A.M. General Thomas Wood's men of the Fourth Corps fired both the pontoon and railroad bridges. For a time, some Confederate artillery flared up in response, and then the firing died down. For the moment, the men beyond the breastworks were too exhausted to fight.

Of course Hood intended to continue the fight. During the hours before midnight, the divisions of Generals Henry Clayton and Carter Stevenson had arrived on the field. Other units that had participated in the battle that afternoon were re-grouped, and the army's artillery was wheeled into position in the dark hours.

Exactly what time Hood intended to renew the battle is uncertain. His first report to the Confederate government, penned on December 11, stated only that during the night of November 30 he ordered the artillery forward to open on the Federals "in the morning, when the attack should be renewed." A longer document written in February 1865, when Hood was in Richmond, Virginia, avoids the subject of a second attack. Hood also avoided the subject in his posthumous reminiscence, *Advance and Retreat*, published in 1880, which said nothing about plans for a second assault. One is inclined to believe that Hood, on the Franklin battlefield, was ready to renew an assault that would have proved as suicidal as the first attack, and gave orders to do so. Later, when the heavy casualty figures were published, Hood downplayed the history of his plans to attack again.

No doubt the orders were given. The only question remains that of timing. General Carter L. Stevenson had brought up the rear in the march of Lee's men to the field. Later he reported that during the night his division was aligned on the Franklin plain "preparatory to an assault which it was announced was to be made by the entire army at daybreak." General Edward C. Walthall of Stewart's Corps recalled more specific instructions. Hood's artillery would open at 7 A.M. and fire one hundred rounds to the gun. At 9 A.M. a general charge would be made by the entire army. If Walthall's record is true, Confederates apparently would have been firing at other Confederates. General James Holtzclaw, a brigade leader in Carter Stevenson's division, reported that his men marched into Franklin shortly after 4 A.M. Meanwhile, General James Chalmers recorded that his men moved forward at "an early hour in the morning" and that his command "was the first to enter the town. . . ."

The conflicting testimony can be resolved. Apparently Hood during the hours before midnight had given orders for a second attack, once Lee's corps and the artillery were on the field. Then, in the early morning hours, it was discovered that Franklin was abandoned. Abandoned, except for the dead and wounded strewn across the field. . . .

Perhaps they were shot down two weeks later in the battle at Nashville, or lived for decades to become members of the United Confederate Veterans, old men with fierce moustaches, canes, and solid opinions. Regardless, they never forgot until the time of their death the scenes of carnage on the Franklin field that morning.

Before the first attack, soldiers of Quarles's brigade in Stewart's corps had come to their chaplain, James M'Neilly, to ask if he would keep treasured items during the battle. According to the chaplain, the men realized that the battle would result in "heavy slaughter" and so brought watches, jewelry, letters, and photographs. They asked that the items be sent home if they were killed.

The field was littered with the dead and wounded of Quarles's brigade and many others. Along the narrow space between the Lewisburg and Carter's Creek pikes lay almost 1,700 Confederate dead. Near the Columbia Pike, where the fighting had been the most severe, the outer ditch was in some places piled seven deep with corpses. The dead, many mangled and blackened by gunsmoke, lay in every grotesque, twisted fashion. Some Confederate dead were found standing upright, their rigid legs jammed between the bodies of comrades. Meanwhile, off beyond the cotton gin, the dead mount of General John Adams remained astraddle the parapet.

Through the cold dawn hours searchers moved through the grisly outer ditch. Some searched for personal friends, dead or alive. Stretcher bearers carried off hundreds of wounded who had suffered through the night. Franklin became one massive field hospital. Churches and homes were filled with the wounded.

Just how many men were lost that afternoon and evening is difficult to ascertain. Certainly General Hood's December 11 message to the government understated the casualty rate when he declared a loss of only 4,500 men. A comparison of Hood's field returns for November 6 and December 10 tells a different story. If one adds to the November 6 return the 3,000 men of Chalmers's and Buford's cavalry divisions not listed there, Hood's "effective total present" was 33,599. Even making no allowances for any casualties in the two cavalry divisions, Hood's "effective total present" on December 10 was only 26,053, a difference of 7,546. General John Schofield's staff accumulated their own statistics when the corps reoccupied Franklin after the battle of Nashville. Schofield's men did a count of graves and found that 1,750 of Hood's men had been buried on the field, 3,800 were so disabled as to be placed in Franklin hospitals, and another 702 were captured. This does not include the wounded who were not hospitalized and thus not left behind in Franklin.

The best summation is that Hood's Franklin losses were about 7,000 men, including 1,750 killed on the field, about 4,500 wounded, and another 702 taken prisoner. For a battle that raged only about five hours, Hood's losses were staggering. He lost at least one-third of the infantry sent into the battle. In the long Seven Days campaign of 1862 in Virginia, General George McClellan's Federal army of 105,445 men fought Robert E. Lee for seven days and suffered a loss of only 1,734 men killed. At Chancellorsville in 1863, the 97,000 men of General Joseph Hooker's Army of the Potomac fought for two days and suffered fewer battle deaths than Hood's 20,000 attackers in five hours at Franklin. The same comparison could be made with much larger armies in other battles that lasted far longer—Grant at Shiloh, Rosecrans at Stone's River and Chickamauga, and others. Even in a Civil War renowned for great carnage, General John Bell Hood at Franklin had slaughtered his army.

★ ★ ★

SOME day large, verdant military parks would protect other battlefields, particularly those on the Virginia front. Huge monuments of bronze, marble, or granite would adorn fields such as Chancellorsville, Gettysburg, and Fredericksburg where men had shed their blood. Today shopping centers, factories, and other marks of modern, commercialized America cover the fields of Franklin where the dead and wounded lay on the morning of December 1.

It was different that cold morning as Hood's army paused to bury the dead. Burial parties labored for two days, digging long trenches. A crude wooden head board marked the site of each man's location, giving as much information as possible.

The winter of 1864–65 was extremely cold in Middle Tennessee. One by one, hundreds of the wood markers were pulled from the earth by people seeking firewood. This troubled Colonel John McGavock, master of Carnton mansion, which stands today just west of the Lewisburg Pike. In April of 1866, McGavock set aside two acres of land adjacent to his family cemetery, only three hundred yards from the Carnton house. Men were hired to seek out the burial trenches. They did not find all of them, but they did bring the remains of 1,481 soldiers to the cedar-lined cemetery. These soldiers were buried by states, as they had been on the original ground. Large rock markers noted the presence of hundreds of Southern boys who rested in unknown graves.

Not all of Franklin's dead were unknown. Fountain Branch Carter and his family emerged from the basement of their home on the morning of December 1. Their unwelcome guest, General Jacob Cox, had long since departed his field headquarters and was en route to Nashville. Behind him, Cox had left incredible scenes of desolation and carnage across the grounds of the Carter home. Among those left behind was young Captain Tod Carter, who lay mortally wounded within a few hundred yards of the family doorstep. A Confederate soldier brought the sad tidings to the family.

The Carnton (John and Randall McGavock) House.
[*Photograph by Rudy E. Sanders.*]

Immediately an elder brother searched the field unsuccessfully for the wounded Tod Carter. While he was gone, General Thomas Benton Smith came to the Carter house and led Fountain Branch Carter and other family members to the wounded boy. Young Tod Carter was lifted gently and taken to die in his boyhood home.

Just across the Columbia Pike, near the cotton gin, other searchers found the body of General Patrick Cleburne. For four years the soldiers of the Army of Tennessee had demonstrated three attitudes for the men who had led them into war. In the case of a General Braxton Bragg, the sentiment had been one of scorn, if not hatred. General Joe Johnston and William J. Hardee had prompted outbursts of respect and affection. For one such as Cleburne, the troops had more a feeling of idolatry. Patrick Cleburne was the idol of his division, if not that of Frank Cheatham's entire corps and perhaps the entire army as well.

Through the night Cleburne's survivors had clung to the outer edge of the parapet. One veteran recalled later that the men waited for Cleburne to give the order for them to attack and charge over the dirt parapet. The attack order never came, and the veteran mused that he *knew* Pat Cleburne was dead because the order never came. Reports circulated through the ranks that night that Cleburne was missing in action. When Cleburne failed to return to the area where his staff watched the battle, the officers became anxious and sent out search parties through the night. One party stumbled upon a Confederate who had been captured and then had escaped across the parapet; he insisted that Cleburne had been captured.

Cleburne's body was discovered near dawn on the morning of December 1. It lay about sixty yards south of the earthworks and about a hundred yards east of the Columbia Pike—almost directly south of the Carter family's cotton gin. Later would come fanciful stories of how Cleburne was shot as his horse leaped astride the earthworks, and how the general was pierced by forty-nine bullets.

John McQuade, one of three soldiers who found the body, recalled that Cleburne lay flat upon his back, the military cap partly over his eyes. He had been shot once, on the left side of his chest. During the night, some ghoul had stripped the General of his boots, watch, sword belt, and other valuables.

Thomas Markham, a chaplain in Featherston's brigade, was another searcher on the field. Markham and some ambulance corpsmen located the body of General John Adams near that of Cleburne. Stewart's and Cleburne's lines had become so entangled during the first attack that the two generals fell almost directly in front of the Carter ginhouse. Adams lay about a hundred yards east of the Columbia Pike, near modern-day Cleburne Avenue. Cleburne's body was sixty yards to the south.

While the corpsmen lifted Adams's body into the ambulance, the soldier John McQuade approached and pointed out Cleburne's body. The ambulance workers immediately lifted the Irishman's corpse into the ambulance. The bodies were taken to Colonel John McGavock's residence at Carnton and were laid out on the lower gallery.

Already the remains of two other generals slain near the Columbia Pike rested on the gallery. General Otho Strahl had perished in the ditch just west of the Columbia Pike, along the route of modern-day Strahl Street. Strahl's body had been carried to the McGavock home during the night. General Hiram Granbury of Cleburne's division had been killed in the ditch to the east, in the vicinity of the Columbia Pike. Early on the morning of December 1, his body was carried to the McGavock home.

Later, tradition would maintain that the bodies of all six generals killed at Franklin rested on the lower gallery of the McGavock home. Research has long since indicated, however, that General John C. Carter was not taken to the McGavock home. In fact, Carter did not perish from his wounds until December 10. On the night of the battle, Carter was taken southward along the Columbia Pike, across Winstead Hill to the Harrison house, where he later died.

A number of writers, accepting Carter's absence from the McGavock home, have asserted that at least a fifth officer, General States Rights Gist, was brought to Carnton. Gist had ridden forward during the first attack, just west of the Columbia Pike. He ordered his men forward, waved his hat to the Twenty-fourth South Carolina Regiment, and rode into the dense smoke. His horse was shot down, and Gist continued on foot, leading the right of his brigade. He was shot through the heart and fell not far from General Strahl.

Slightly over ten years ago, some careful research by Howell and Elizabeth Purdue indicated that Gist's body was not taken to the

General Hiram B. Granbury.

Carnton, showing the porch where the bodies of several dead Confederate generals were placed after the Battle of Franklin.

[*Photograph by Rudy E. Sanders.*]

---

The Confederate Cemetery where more than 1,400 soldiers are buried.▶

[*Photograph by Rudy E. Sanders.*]

C.M.B. STREET
SERGT MAJOR
9ª MISS REGT
KILLED
Nov. 30. 1864
AT
FRANKLIN. TENN.

McGavock home. The researchers located an account of Gist's burial as described by his body servant, "Uncle Wiley" Howard of South Carolina. According to the servant's account, the wounded general was taken to a field hospital on the far left of the Confederate line. Gist died there on the night of November 30. The next morning, the faithful servant remained with the corpse as it was taken to the residence of William White, where Gist was buried in the yard under a large cedar tree. According to the researchers, the house where Gist died was on the far western side of the battlefield, almost two miles west of the Carter house. The William White home fronted on the Boyd Mill Road.

Across the field, the John McGavock home was packed with the dead and wounded. On the lower gallery, field surgeons worked near the bodies of the four dead general officers. The rooms of the spacious home were filled with suffering men. One onlooker, chaplain James M'Neilly of Quarles's brigade, suffered in his own way. He had worked all night at a field hospital located behind General A.P. Stewart's lines, doing what he could to assist the field surgeons. Someone came and told M'Neilly that his brother had been killed near the Carter cotton gin. The sad M'Neilly could do nothing to find his brother in the darkness and worked through the night at the hospital. At dawn he walked across the field, from the railroad cut by the Lewisburg Pike across Stewart's and Cleburne's front to the vicinity of the cotton gin. "I could have trodden on a dead man at every step. . . . The dead were piled up in the trenches almost to the top of the earthworks," the chaplain remembered. He walked past the dead mount of General John Adams, which remained atop the earthworks. The sad mission was soon over. M'Neilly found his brother's body close to where General Patrick Cleburne lay. Then M'Neilly sadly walked to the McGavock house.

In the house, ladies of Franklin ministered to the wounded. Casualties were so heavy that the outbuildings of the Carnton mansion were also pressed into service for hospital use. Mrs. John McGavock, mistress of Carnton, supervised the makeshift nursing care. She also took pains to care for the personal items of General Cleburne that had not been stolen on the battlefield—his cap, sword, and other effects. Today the cap Cleburne wore is preserved in the Tennessee State Museum.

Through the morning a sad procession of Cleburne's men

came to the McGavock home for one last view of their beloved commander. Then the bodies of Cleburne, Granbury, and a colonel of the latter's brigade were placed in an ambulance for a long drive to Columbia, Tennessee. In the late morning, the body of General Otho Strahl and two junior officers had been sent off on the same route, down modern-day U.S. Highway 31.

On a cold December 2, the body of General Strahl was interred in Columbia's Rose Hill Cemetery. A few hours later, funeral services were read for Cleburne, Granbury, and Colonel Young in the parlor of the William Polk home at Columbia, where they had lain in state the previous night. These three officers were then buried near General Strahl.

The choice of burial sites troubled the prominent Army of Tennessee chaplain (later Bishop) Charles Quintard. In his diary for December 3 Quintard expressed his dissatisfaction with the sexton's placement of the graves because they were close to the graves of Union soldiers. Chaplain Quintard made arrangements for the bodies to be removed to St. John's Episcopal Church, on modern-day U.S. Highway 43 between Columbia and Mt. Pleasant.

St. John's was an especially fitting resting place for General Patrick Cleburne. On the march from Florence, Alabama, to Columbia, prior to the disasters at Spring Hill and Franklin, Cleburne's division marched along the pike past the church. Cleburne reined in and admired the gothic beauty of the vine-clad structure. He turned, as previously noted, to one of his staff officers and remarked that it was almost worth dying for, "to be buried in such a beautiful spot."

It was an appropriate resting place for any soldier of the Army of Tennessee. St. John's, consecrated in 1842, had been built by the late Bishop-General Leonidas Polk and his family, on a plot of ground across the pike from the manor of Ashwood Hall. Polk had died in the Georgia campaign, but his nephew, General Lucius Polk, was in Columbia and selected the gravesites for the Confederate officers. Lucius Polk, the plantation lord, and Patrick Cleburne, the Irish immigrant, had fought together in the bloody battle at Chickamauga and many other campaigns.

By December 5, General Patrick Cleburne rested in the quiet cemetery at St. John's. That afternoon, far to the south, his fiancée walked in the garden of her family's home in Mobile, Alabama. Susan Tarleton fainted when she heard a newsboy cry on a nearby street the tidings of the battle at Franklin and Patrick Cleburne's death.

★ ★ ★

THE tormented John Bell Hood was inclined to let the dead bury the dead. By 1 P.M. on December 1, General Stephen Lee's corps had moved past the ambulance attendants and gravediggers en route to Nashville. Stewart's and Cheatham's corps followed on December 2. Hood's depleted army trudged northward along the Nashville Pike and took position on the hills south of the city. It was a ghost army. The muster rolls now listed only 18,702 infantry as "effective total present." The officer ranks had been decimated. A colonel was the ranking leader in General John C. Brown's division. In Stewart's corps alone, three brigade and twenty-four regimental commanders had been killed, wounded, or captured at Franklin.

It was the last act of a once-great army that had struck fear into the hearts of enemies during better times, at Shiloh, Perryville, Chickamauga, and elsewhere. Now it was something quixotic and out of a past not far gone yet very distant. The last of the generals and infantry, artillery, and ramshackle wagons moved across the Harpeth River. Like a ghost from the past, the Army of Tennessee had loomed up suddenly out of the depths of the Deep South. The army of great legends and people of legends—Albert Sidney Johnston, Bishop Polk, Patrick Cleburne, and others—the last remnants of western Confederate power—it had come to this. Thin ranks of proud officers and determined men, short on guns, food, wagons, every need of a military force, shivered in the cold December weather along the hills south of Nashville. In the city, the streets were alive with columns of blue infantry, busy steamboat wharves, factories, and mountains of supplies.

While Hood urged his men onward toward Nashville, a huge military force was assembling in the city. At the battle of Franklin, General John Schofield's casualties numbered 2,326. On December 10, Schofield's army, safely within the confines of Nashville's defenses, listed 24,600 men present for duty. In addition, General George Thomas was accumulating a massive body of men at Nashville: General A.J. Smith's brigades from Missouri, Wilson's cavalry and troops from outposts in Middle Tennessee. The

Civil War had come to something that John Bell Hood never understood, something beyond the realm of frenetic foxchases while a Kentucky youth, or the glitter of ballroom promenades while the lion of society in a Richmond of 1863. The war was men and material by late 1864. The weapons and ammunition were there in plenty, stored alongside the tracks of the Louisville and Nashville Railroad or along the wharves covering lower Broad Street. The men were in abundance. By the second week of December, Thomas had accumulated a force of over 70,000 men within Nashville's earthworks. The earthworks themselves gave evidence that the war had changed from the type Hood had always envisioned. As the late Stanley Horn observed in his classic work, *The Army of Tennessee*, Nashville was perhaps the most heavily fortified city on the American continent. A strong inner line of breastworks, supported by several forts and twenty artillery batteries, extended in an arc from the Cumberland River above the town to the river's edge below. A much longer line, perhaps over thirteen miles in length, extended through the modern residential part of Nashville, again from the river above to the stream below the town. Nashville was impregnable, garrisoned by a huge force at least three times the size of Hood's army.

From Hood's statements preserved in the National Archives and the *War of the Rebellion: A Compilation of the Official Records of the Union and Confederate Armies*, it is clear that the hapless officer did not know that Thomas's army was at Nashville. Hood rode to Nashville amid the delusion that great events still might occur north of the Ohio River. There is little to indicate that Hood could have known of Thomas's troops, save that he had received intelligence by December 6 that 15,000 Federal troops were en route to Nashville from the Mississippi valley. Hood was a dealer in dreams, and now he played out his last hand in the careless fashion that had characterized his military career. Years after the war, Hood's memoir, *Advance and Retreat*, attempted to leave the impression that the general was well aware of the circumstances. Hood argued later that he was cognizant of Thomas's strength at Nashville. According to the memoir, Hood knew of Thomas's power, of the miles of entrenchments, and so on. He intended to encamp in the Nashville hills, await reinforcement from across the Mississippi River, and force General George Thomas to move out and attack him.

All of this is sheer hindsight. Hood's dispatches and reports, now preserved in the manuscript files of the National Archives and in the *Official Records,* indicate that the general moved northward from Franklin into a veritable trap, knowing nothing of Thomas's strength at Nashville. Hood's obsession was two-fold—to catch up with Schofield and to penetrate the mystic region of the Ohio River. His claim to be awaiting reinforcements from across the Mississippi was illusionary. Hood had not received the slightest indication from the government that such troops could be sent.

Other matters indicate that he was living in a dream world, torn somewhere between the realities of the cold Nashville hills and the memory of war in Virginia during the more romantic days.

Still, Hood wanted to be a Lee, but he lacked that officer's character. The deluded Hood issued congratulations to the army on December 1 for the "victory" of the previous day. On December 3, he reported to Richmond that a victory had been gained at Franklin—but mentioned nothing of his losses save the casualties in the officer ranks. On December 5, Hood reported to Richmond again. He did not mention the general casualty figures but said only that the loss of officers was "excessively large in proportion to the loss of men."

The government would not learn the truth until February 1865, when Hood filed his final report of the Tennessee campaign. The document, filled with explanations of failure allegedly caused by other officers, nonetheless recounted the end of the Army of Tennessee. On December 15–16, 1864, General George Thomas's massive force moved in mechanical fashion out of the Nashville earthworks to contend with Hood's thin lines. It was no contest, because the disparity in numbers was overwhelming. The Federals, with excellent execution, hurled more troops against the Confederate left flank than Hood had in his whole army. On the gray afternoon of December 16, Hood's lines, stretched beyond endurance, finally gave way.

Bate's regiments atop Shy's Hill were practically annihilated, and the remnants of Cheatham's Corps fled for the Granny White Pike. When they realized that General James Wilson's troop-

---

Masonic Hall, which was used for barracks and as a hospital by the armies.

*[Photograph by Rudy E. Sanders.]*

ers blocked their line of retreat, Cheatham's units went totally to pieces, melting into a disorganized rabble that threw away small arms, abandoned artillery, and scurried for the Franklin Pike, a little farther to the east and parallel to the Granny White. Stewart's corps was caught up in the rout as well.

Only Lee's corps retained any organization. Shocked to see the army evaporating before his eyes, Lee skillfully pulled back his troops to the Overton Hills. While a young drummer beat the long roll, Lee held firm until his entire corps could be placed in retreat. Yet the end had come so quickly that sixteen of Lee's guns were captured before the artillery horses could be brought up from the rear. For the most part, the broken remnants of a once great army scrambled through the Overton Hills and struggled southward, the vanguard crossing the Harpeth River on December 17.

They came back to Franklin as a cold December rain fell across the Nashville Pike and on their broken dreams. There the suffering continued. The little town on the banks of the Harpeth still presented a sad spectacle. The courthouse, the churches, the Franklin Female Institute, the Masonic Hall, and many homes were yet filled with the wounded. Just as at Nashville, the weather had been extremely cold, with snow, sleet, and ice. "It was the most terrible spell of weather I ever knew," H.P. Figuers wrote later. At the time of the battle Figuers was a fifteen-year-old boy who lived in a big house facing the Carter's Creek Pike, the house that Federal General William Grose used as his headquarters. Figuers had watched the two armys taking position, first from a vantage point atop the barn, and later, part of the time, from the boughs of one of two large oak trees in the front yard (the house and the oaks still stand). When the battle had started, the boy remained near the house while his mother and the other children sought safety closer in town at a friend's home. Soon a number of wounded Confederate prisoners had been sent into the house and Figuers recalled that, unsuccessful in his efforts to secure a doctor, he "made up fires, found pillows, and made them all as comfortable as possible by making pallets on the floor and dressing their wounds as best I could."

Soon after midnight, when the fighting had ceased, Figuers's mother had returned home and taken charge of caring for the wounded. In fact, she also took responsibility for the wounded in the nearby Episcopal church. Figuers remembered that the soldiers began calling her "Little Mother." Finding sufficient food for so many men was a problem. "Many a day," Figuers wrote, "I went out through the country in an old dump cart hunting for food. We would take a large wash kettle, holding about twenty gallons," he continued, "and make it full of soup with plenty of red pepper. For this soup I brought in from the country Irish potatoes, cabbage, dried beans, and turnips, and in making it we used any kind of meat obtainable. The soldiers thought this was great diet; in fact, the best they had had for more than a year."

A young girl in Franklin, a student at the Female Institute, had similar experiences caring for the wounded. She later remembered that school was disrupted for some time after the battle. "Our house was full as could be" with the wounded, she wrote; and "from morning until night we made bandages and scraped linen lint with which to dress the wounds, besides making jellies and soups with which to nourish them."

One of the most interesting and detailed accounts was left by Dr. Deering J. Roberts, a Confederate surgeon, who was in charge of caring for the wounded of Bate's division. "I found an old carriage-and wagon-shop about sixty by one hundred feet, two stories high," the doctor related. "It had a good roof, plenty of windows above and below, an incline leading up to the upper floor on the outside, and a good well. This I immediately placarded as 'Bate's Division Hospital,' and put part of the detail to work cleaning out the work-benches, old lumber, and other debris." The doctor said that in his hospital, while at Franklin, only seven men died: two from abdominal wounds, three from gunshot wounds in the head, one with amputation of the thigh, and one who refused to submit to amputation. "I never amputated a limb without consent of the wounded man," explained Roberts. "Despite all arguments and reasoning, this man refused amputation, was greatly depressed and despondent from the first, and died on December 23, as I had expected, from a gunshot injury to the forearm. . . ."

Now as the Confederates, defeated at Nashville, retreated through Franklin, all the soldiers who were able to endure being removed were taken out, but the more unfortunate had to remain and be captured. A few days after the Federals reoccupied the town, railroad traffic was renewed and the wounded, according to young Figuers, "were taken away in open rack cars, such as cattle are now shipped in. Only a few of them had overcoats or blankets, the weather was dreadfully cold, and their suffering was indescrib-

From the branches of one of these giant oak trees fifteen–year–old Hardin
Perkins Figuers watched the Battle of Franklin.

[*Photograph by Rudy E. Sanders.*]

The Williamson County Court House served as a hospital following
the battle.

[*Photograph by Rudy E. Sanders.*]

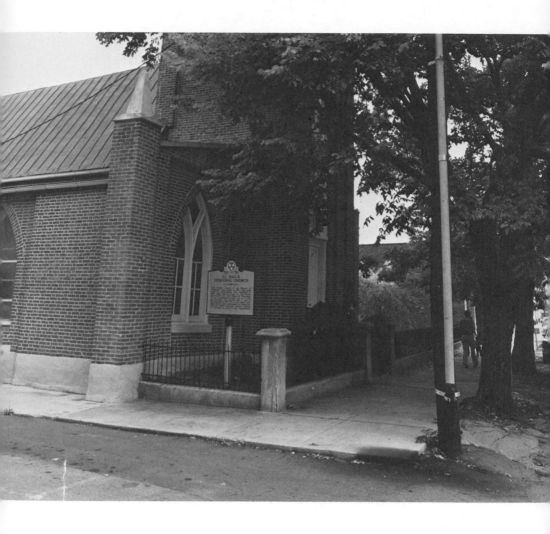

St. Paul's Episcopal Church was used as a hospital following the battle, first by Confederates, later by the Federals. It is said that after the war the basement was a meeting place for women who sewed uniforms for the Ku Klux Klan.

[*Photograph by Rudy E. Sanders.*]

able." Particularly Figuers remembered Colonel William L. Butler, Twenty-eighth Alabama, who was in his mother's house, "desperately wounded," shot "clean through from side to side." Nevertheless, a Federal surgeon pronounced Butler sufficiently recovered to be sent to prison, which was done despite Butler's vehement protests.

One of the Federals coming back into Franklin was W.A. Keesy, Sixty-fourth Ohio, who vividly testified of the awful scenes of suffering. Anxious to find "some of our missing boys," he went to the hospitals at the first chance he got. "The store buildings were turned into hospitals and were filled with both Union and Confederate wounded," he remembered. "On coming to the first hospital I was confronted on the porch with men terribly wounded. As a sample, one man, shot through the jaw, his tongue protruding out of his mouth, rested his head upon his hands. He could not speak. Another was shot in the thigh, but able to be laid out on the porch, although he was badly doubled up. I went into the room which was perhaps one hundred feet long," Keesy continued. "The men . . . were laid with their heads to the wall and their feet toward the center of the room, leaving aisles between the feet of the two rows and next to the walls at their heads," he said. "These had all been lying there during the two weeks in which we had been campaigning, on the bare floor."

Stepping into the room Keesy detected, "at once, a sickening, poisonous atmosphere that seemed to suffocate me. I supposed I could soon overcome this, and pressed on; but by the time I had gotten ten feet into the room I found that I had none too much time left if I would get out before fainting. I hurried out without getting a chance to speak to anyone, or anyone speaking to me. The stench arising from the putrifying wounds was really unbearable." Next the Union soldier went out to the battlefield, to the line of works, still filled with evidence of carnage. "As I stood there and thought of the awful suffering and slaughter of the battle, and how nearly I had come to being one of the number to inhabit the ditches," he said that he trembled.

★ ★ ★

THERE would be no stand at Columbia as Hood had envisioned. The road from Nashville was strewn with abandoned wagons, artillery, baggage, and small arms. Thousands of men were bare-foot and dressed in thin clothing. With a rearguard commanded by Forrest, the army marched on to the Tennessee River, bound for Hood's supply bases at Tupelo and Corinth. On the retreat Forrest returned once more to Beechlawn, the Warfield home just south of Columbia, where earlier, during the Confederate advance, the library reportedly had been the scene of a dispute between Hood and Forrest about the strategy of the campaign. Forrest did not stay long, and the very next day Schofield is said to have arrived, his troops allegedly taking every ham in the smokehouse, every chicken, and every fence rail. But later, when Major Amos Warfield fell into Federal hands, General Schofield personally intervened to guarantee that the Confederate officer was returned home safely.

The weather, after a brief moderation, changed again on December 21, and a driving snow pelted the miserable Confederate column while icy roads slashed the bare feet of thousands. On Christmas Day they began crossing the Tennessee River near Florence. Efforts by the Confederate government to learn the truth from General Hood were unsuccessful until Lieutenant General Richard Taylor visited the army on January 9. Only then did Beauregard learn that Hood had no more than fifteen thousand infantrymen remaining with the army. Of these, fewer than half were still equipped or considered effective. By January 14, when Beauregard arrived at Tupelo, the army was practically without food and still had no winter clothing and few blankets to withstand the unusually cold Mississippi winter. The day before Beauregard arrived, Hood applied to the government to be relieved from command. Two days later Richmond formally authorized Beauregard to replace Hood with Taylor.

# EPILOGUE

THE BLOODY HOLOCAUST at Franklin, never transcended as tragic drama even by such legendary struggles as Shiloh or Chickamauga, Antietam or Spotsylvania, long continued to be a story in irony, never to be generally recognized by the nation for what it was: a massive slaughter and the death-knell of a once mighty army. Soon after the end of the war, General George H. Thomas told J.T. Trowbridge, author of *The South: A Tour of Its Battlefields and Ruined Cities*, that several national soldiers' cemeteries had been proposed by him and sanctioned by the War Department. Thomas assured Trowbridge that there would be a national cemetery for the Franklin battlefield. Through the years the proposal for a national cemetery at Franklin came up again and again. Many people worked hard to make it a reality. Senators and congressmen were enlisted to exert their influence in achieving the goal. At times there were encouraging statements from those in responsible positions. For instance, Secretary of War J.M. Dickinson once said that there was as much reason for establishing a national military park at Franklin as at Chickamauga-Chattanooga and Shiloh. But "the bottom line," finally, was that the United States Congress simply was not willing to appropriate the necessary money for another military park.

By 1910, former Confederate General George W. Gordon, the same who was captured by the Federals at Franklin, was a member of the U.S. House of Representatives. In a letter of that year addressed to Mrs. N.B. Dozier, one of the persons who worked diligently for a national park and cemetery, Gordon succintly summarized the fate of the project. First assuring the lady that her efforts "meet with my heartiest sympathy," Mr. Gordon then said that the Committee on Military Affairs was "not favorably disposed" toward granting the $100,000 requested. The bill had been laid aside, seeming "to have but little favor."

[ 179

The Marshall House, built in 1809, had its eighteen-inch-thick brick wall penetrated by an iron cannon ball during the Battle of Franklin.
[*Photograph by Rudy E. Sanders.*]

◄Franklin's Monument to the Confederate soldiers.
[*Photograph by Rudy E. Sanders.*]

Even in the late 1920s some people were still trying to get a national park at Franklin, but actually nothing had changed since General Gordon penned his letter to Mrs. Dozier. So far as the United States government was concerned, Franklin remained uncommemorated.

For a while though, it seemed likely that the battle would be brought to national attention in another manner. In 1923 Hollywood's Metro Pictures Corporation—afterward Metro-Goldwyn-Mayer—came to Franklin. A movie to be entitled *The Human Mill*, a screen adaptation of John Trotwood Moore's nostalgic novel of the Old South, *The Bishop of Cottontown,* was to be climaxed with a largescale reenactment of the fierce struggle of November 30, 1864. Directed by a young man with a brilliant reputation, Allen Holubar, the project fired the imagination of thousands. In fact, Holubar, from his Hermitage Hotel "command post" in Nashville, announed that at least four thousand men (more than Franklin's entire population in 1923) would be required for the movie. People responded by the thousands. Even hundreds of ex-servicemen— veterans of Chateau-Thierry and the Argonne—came to participate.

On the day of the filming, September 27, several special trains, packed with volunteer warriors, pulled into Franklin. Estimates of those who came merely to watch were placed as high as ten thousand. They gathered on a part of the actual battlefield, the filming area located approximately a mile south of the town, west of and some half mile off the Columbia Pike. There a crew had worked for several days, digging trenches, stringing rail fences, burying hundreds of mines designed to simulate artillery fire. At last, despite such aggravations as traffic "backed up for miles," most participants demanding a Confederate uniform, and outbreaks of premature firing, the great moment arrived. The filming began and the "actors" went about their work with zest. The noise, the smoke, and the action were captivating. The hand-to-hand fighting that developed quickly became—thought some—more real than simulated. The clash of battle was too much for one Confederate guest of honor. Behind the restraining ropes of the spectator area he scuffled feebly with a guard. "Let me at 'em, boy!"

Confederate Veterans, Company B, First Tennessee, in the 1920s.

he shouted. "I fit 'em here in '64, and I ain't afeared to fight 'em now!"

When five hundred feet of battle scenes had been filmed, Holubar stopped the cameras. He leaped down from his stand exultant. "Those were great battle scenes," exclaimed the pleased director. "Let the buglers sound 'Cease Firing.' " The buglers blew—and blew and blew. But the "battle" continued. Holubar stalked up and down, waving his arms and shouting: "Stop it! Stop it! The battle's over!" Some witnesses thought it was fifteen minutes before the action was finally ended.

It all seemed very promising, but movieland's version of the battle of Franklin followed the same script as the movement for a national park, never materializing. Within weeks after the battle scenes were filmed, director Holubar was dead. Word from his colleagues was that his reenactment of the battle had proved to be masterful, some of the best battle scenes ever filmed. Nevertheless, the company was apparently unwilling to entrust the remainder of the filming to some other person. Half finished, *The Human Mill* was stored and forgotten, according to some accounts ultimately perishing in a fire years later.

* * *

VETERANS of November 30, 1864, came back to Franklin upon many occasions, sometimes in small groups, or even alone; sometimes for full-scale reunions. One such grand occasion was in September 1887. Confederate veterans from all over the South, with family and friends, poured into Franklin on every train that arrived. Not since the war itself had the town seen such a gathering of soldiers in gray. Newspapers were filled with accounts of the campaign and battle and plans for the parade through the streets of Franklin and out to the cemetery at McGavock's Grove.

The parade, with people lining the streets as many businesses closed their doors for the event, began soon after nine o'clock in the morning of Friday, September 23, with bands playing "Dixie" and other appropriate selections, and finally moved through the town to the grove and cemetery. Captain H. A. Tyler, who had ridden with Forrest, Captain John W. Morton, Chief of Artillery in Forrest's cavalry, and Lieutenant Mark Cockrill were among those who spoke to the veterans and friends, almost in the shadow of the Carnton mansion where the bodies of Cleburne, Adams, Strahl, and Granbury had been brought when the battle had ended.

Probably the greatest gathering of veterans in the twentieth century was on the fiftieth anniversary of the battle. To the strains of "Dixie" were added "Yankee Doodle" and other patriotic songs, as the trains brought Union as well as Confederate veterans to Franklin for the observance. There was even a special train from Nashville carrying prominent veterans of both sides. Around the square and through the principal streets they marched. Speeches were made by such people as Confederate Colonel Robert W. Banks of Mississippi and Federal Colonel Isaac R. Sherwood of Ohio, while poet and author John Trotwood Moore of Tennessee read a poem entitled "Reunited." Then there was a dinner for more than a thousand people at the courthouse, followed by a visit to the cemetery at Carnton.

By then, of course, much had changed. Some prominent landmarks were no longer extant. The old Carter cotton gin, for instance, had been gone for years. In fact, Colonel Moscow Carter, surviving his father, had sold the home place and moved to Triune nearly twenty years earlier. The ranks of the veterans had dwindled steadily. Generals Hood and Forrest had both been dead for more than three decades. Emerson Opdycke had perished from a self-inflicted, although accidental, gunshot wound in 1884. Schofield had been dead since 1906. Many, many veterans had long been dead when the fiftieth anniversary reunion was held in 1914.

But some of the veterans, a precious few, continued to return to the tragic site at Franklin as long as they could struggle onto a train, or into an automobile. There is a picture taken in the 1920s, showing a small group of survivors from Company B, First Tennessee Infantry, gathered in front of the Pension Office in Nashville. Dressed in their gray uniforms they stand proud but feeble, the last few of a generation whose niche in American history is incomparable; a generation that lives now only in literature—and legend.

# NOTES

## CHAPTER 1

For information on Hood's personality and background, see Thomas L. Connelly, *Autumn of Glory: The Army of Tennessee, 1862–1865* (Baton Rouge, 1971), 321–23, 429–32, 503–4, 506–7. Biographical information on Hood's career is available in John P. Dyer, *The Gallant Hood* (Indianapolis, 1950), and in Richard McMurry, *John Bell Hood and the War for Southern Independence* (Lexington, Ky., 1982). For information on Atlanta casualties, see Connelly, *Autumn of Glory*, 388–89, 437, 444, 450, 455, 467; other documentary information is available in Jefferson Davis Papers, Tulane University; Braxton Bragg Papers, Western Reserve Historical Society; John Bell Hood Papers, National Archives; *War of the Rebellion: A Compilation of the Official Records of the Union and Confederate Armies* (73 vols., Washington, D.C., 1880–1901), XXXVIII, pt. 3, 677–79 (hereinafter cited as *OR*). For information on command friction in the Army of Tennessee after the Atlanta campaign, see Connelly, *Autumn of Glory*, 470–73; Hood to Braxton Bragg, Sept. 4, 1864, in Jefferson Davis Papers, Duke University; William J. Hardee to wife, Aug. 17, 1864, in William J. Hardee Papers, Alabama State Department of Archives and History; Hood to Bragg, Sept. 5, 1864, in Hood Cipher Book, II, Hood Papers, National Archives; Stanley F. Horn, *The Army of Tennessee* (Norman, Okla., 1955), 362. The confusion regarding the constantly changing grand strategy of the campaign is discussed in Connelly, *Autumn of Glory*, 472–92; Thomas Robson Hay, *Hood's Tennessee Campaign* (New York, 1929), 37–76; Horn, *Army of Tennessee*, 374–83; T. Harry Williams, *P.G.T. Beauregard, Napoleon in Gray* (Baton Rouge, 1955), 241–43; Alfred Roman, *The Military Operations of General Beauregard in the War Between the States, 1861 to 1865* (2 vols., New York, 1883), 2: 277–81; John Bell Hood, *Advance and Retreat: Personal Experiences in the United States and Confederate States Armies,* ed. Richard Current (Bloomington, 1959), 262–63, 258, 270, 268, 366–67; Jefferson Davis to Beauregard, Oct. 2, 1864, Francis Shoup Journal, Sept. 10, 14, 19, 29–Oct. 6, Oct. 10–13, 15–16, Nov. 24–27, 1864; Beauregard to Hood, Nov. 15, 1864, in Telegrams Received Hood's Command,

National Archives; Jefferson Davis to Beauregard, November 1, 1864, Davis to Hood, November 7, 1864, in Beauregard Letters, University of Texas Library; *OR*, XXXIX, pt. 2, 862, 864, pt. 1, 803, pt. 3, 804, 831, 835, 797, 870–71, 858, 879, 882–83, 887, 891, 904, 908, 917–18, XLV, pt. 1, 1220, 1224, 1214; W.T. Walthall to S.D. Lee, Nov. 17, 1879, in Stephen D. Lee Papers, University of North Carolina; T.B. Roy Sketch of General William J. Hardee, in Hardee Papers, Alabama.

CHAPTER 2

For information on Sherman's plans to march to the Atlantic and their bearing on General Thomas and the defense of Middle Tennessee, see *OR*, XXXIX, pt. 2, 355–56, 364, 413, pt. 3, 3, 162, 202, 222, 239–40, 378, 477, 494, 498, 509, 514–15, 531, 534, 537, 746. Biographical information on Sherman's career is available in Lloyd Lewis, *Sherman, Fighting Prophet* (New York, 1932), and in Basil H. Liddell-Hart, *Sherman, Soldier, Realist, American* (New York, 1929). Biographical sources on Thomas's personality and background are Freeman Cleaves, *Rock of Chickamauga: The Life Of General George H. Thomas* (Norman, Okla., 1948); Francis McKinney, *Education in Violence: The Life of George H. Thomas* (Detroit, 1961); Wilbur D. Thomas, *General George H. Thomas, the Indomitable Warrior* (New York, 1964); and Thomas V. Van Horne, *The Life of Major General George H. Thomas* (New York, 1882). The section on the personality and career of Schofield was developed from the collection of the general's papers in the Library of Congress and from his memoir, *Forty Six Years in the Army* (New York, 1897), 1–15, 61–64, 75–88, 156–58, 226–28, 467–512. Also see James L. McDonough, *Schofield: Union General in the Civil war and Reconstruction* (Tallahassee, Fl., 1972), 1–10, 29–41, 69, 189–92; James L. McDonough, "John McAllister Schofield," *Civil War Times Illustrated*, XIII (August 1974), 10–17; Russell F. Weigley, "The Military Thought of John M. Schofield," *Military Affairs*, XXII and XXIII (1958–59), 77–84. For the discussion of the campaign from Pulaski, Tenn. to Columbia see *OR*, XLV, pt. 1, 340, 752, 885, 956–58, 974, 1000, 1016, 1018, 1020, 1021, 1036, 1085, 1108, XXXIX, pt. 3, 708, 768. Consult also Hay, *Hood's Tennessee Campaign*, 77–82; Connelly, *Autumn of Glory*, 490–93; Horn, *Army of Tennessee*, 383–85; and Campbell H. Brown, "To Rescue the Confederacy," *Civil War Times Illustrated*, Special Nashville Edition (December 1964), 44.

On the relationship between Schofield and Stanley, see David S. Stanley, *Personal Memoirs of Major General D.S. Stanley, U.S.A.* (Cambridge, Mass., 1917), 214. For biographical information on Cox, see Mark M. Boatner III, *The Civil War Dictionary* (New York, 1959), 205–6; Adam Weaver's letter appeared in the *Franklin Review Appeal*, Nov. 27, 1880.

Chapter 3

For information on the Van Dorn murder see Robert G. Hartje, *Van Dorn: The Life and Times of a Confederate General* (Nashville, 1967), 307–27. For some of the "explanations" of Confederate failure at Spring Hill, see accounts in Brown, "To Rescue the Confederacy," 48; Henry Stone, "The Battle of Franklin," in *Papers of the Military Historical Society of Massachusetts, Campaigns in Kentucky and Tennessee* (Boston, 1908), VII, 462–63; and J.D. Remington, "The Cause of Hood's Failure at Spring Hill," *Confederate Veteran* (hereinafter cites as *CV*), XXI (1913), 569–71. On contrasting interpretations of Confederate opportunites at Spring Hill see Bruce Catton, *Never Call Retreat* (New York, 1965), 409, and Stanley F. Horn, "The Spring Hill Legend," *Civil War Times Illustrated*, VIII (April 1969), 20–32. Biographical information on Cheatham came from Clement Evans, ed., *Confederate Military History* (12 vols., Atlanta, 1899); the Joe Spence Diary, 1861–62, Confederate Collection, Tennessee State Library and Archives, Nashville; and Christopher Losson, "Major General Benjamin Franklin Cheatham and the Battle of Stone's River," *Tennessee Historical Quarterly*, XLI (Fall 1982), 278–92. For Wilson's personality and career see McDonough, *Schofield*, 106, 107, 116, 145; James H. Wilson, *Under the Old Flag* (2 vols., New York, 1912), 2: 115, 116; James H. Wilson, *The Life of John A. Rawlings* (New York, 1916), 171–73; Stephen Z. Starr, *The Union Cavalry in the Civil War* (2 vols., Baton Rouge, 1979–81), 1: 5–6. Also consult James Pickett Jones, *Yankee Blitzkrieg: Wilson's Raid through Alabama and Georgia* (Athens, Ga., 1976), and Edward G. Longacre, *From Union Stars to Top Hat* (Harrisburg, Pa., 1972), for additional background material on Wilson.

On the confusion and perplexity of the Spring Hill episode, see *OR*, XLV, pt. 1, 113–15, 147–48, 229, 341–42, 403, 652–53, 708, 736, 742, 752–54, 763–64, 1106–10, 1137, 1141–43, 1150–51, 1169; Connelly, *Autumn of Glory*, 490–502; McDonough, *Schofield*, 105–14, Horn, *Army of*

Tennessee, 385–93; Hay, *Hood's Tennessee Campaign*, 82–85; Jacob D. Cox, *The Battle of Franklin, Tennessee, November 30, 1864* (New York, 1897), 21–28; William M. Wherry, "The Franklin Campaign," in the Schofield Papers, Library of Congress; and Horn, "The Spring Hill Legend," 20–32. Compare and contrast Hood's account in his memoir with B. F. Cheatham, "The Lost Opportunity at Spring Hill—General Cheatham's Reply to General Hood," *Southern Historical Society Papers*, IX (1881), 524–25; also with J.P. Young, "Hood's Failure at Spring Hill," *CV*, XVI (Jan. 1908), 27–31. Finally, Captain H. A. Tyler's reminiscences about Forrest at Spring Hill are found in *CV*, XXII (1914), 15.

CHAPTER 4

For sources on the initial disposition of Hood's troops as they approached Franklin, see various Confederates reports in *OR*, XLV, pt. 1, 653, 670–71, 687, 693, 697, 708, 720, 731, 736, 753–54; Sims Crownover, *The Battle of Franklin* (Nashville, 1955), 11–14; Robert Selph Henry, *"First with the Most" Forrest* (Indianapolis, 1944), 398–99; Howell and Elizabeth Purdue, *Pat Cleburne, Confederate General* (Hillsboro, Tex., 1973), 414–17; Irving A. Buck, *Cleburne and His Command*, ed. Thomas R. Hay (Jackson, Tenn., 1959), 279–81. For sources on Hood's motives for the attack, see Connelly, *Autumn of Glory*, 430–32, 503–4; Hood, *Advance and Retreat*, 162, 292, 294, 297, 81; D.C. Govan to George A. Williams, June ___, 1906, in Buck, *Cleburne and His Command*, 270, Govan to Irving A. Buck, Sept. 3, 1907, *ibid.*, 290. For Hood's references to the cowardice of his troops in previous battles, see Connelly, *Autumn of Glory*, 432, 470, 503–4; Hood to Bragg, Sept. 4, 1864, in Jefferson Davis Papers, Duke; Hood to Bragg, Sept. 5, 1864, in Hood Cipher Book II, Hood Papers, National Archives; Hood, *Advance and Retreat*, 292, 294, 290, 162, 181. For information on General Patrick Cleburne's attitude prior to the battle, see Purdue and Purdue, *Pat Cleburne*, 414–15, 417, 420; Buck, *Cleburne and His Command*, 277–78, 281, 290. For information on the status of Nashville during the Civil War, see Thomas L. Connelly, *Army of the Heartland: the Army of Tennessee, 1861–1862* (Baton Rouge, 1967), 73; F. Garvin Davenport, *Cultural Life in Nashville on the Eve of the Civil War* (Chapel Hill, 1941), 32–55, 117–44, 145–59, 199–210; Alfred L. Crabb, "Twilight of the Nashville Gods," *Tennessee Historical Quarterly*, XV (Dec. 1956), 291–99; Stanley F. Horn, "Nashville During the Civil War," *ibid*, IV (March 1945), 3–22. For information on Schofield's general dispositions and the topography of the battlefield along Hood's approach, see Crownover, *Battle of Franklin*, 11–13; Hay, *Hood's Tennessee Campaign*, 117–20; Horn, *Army of Tennessee*, 395–98; *OR*, XLV, pt. 1, 342, 348–51, 195, 208, 214, 429–30, 365, 742, 653; Purdue and Purdue, *Pat Cleburne*, 418–19, 427; Hood, *Advance and Retreat*, 292–94, 297, 290, 162, 181.

CHAPTER 5

For the Ellison Capers account, consult *OR*, XLV, pt. 1, 737. The Federal officer quoted, as he watched the Confederate advance, is Levi T. Schofield, *The Retreat from Pulaski to Nashville* (Cleveland, 1909), 18. On the problems Schofield confronted at Franklin, see McDonough, *Schofield*, 115; Cox, *Battle of Franklin*, 39. Relative to Schofield's concern for his left flank, upstream on the Harpeth River, see *OR*, XLV, pt. 1, 1170, 1178. For information on Wagner's division being positioned in front of the main Federal line, see *OR*, XLV, pt. 1, 115, 231, 240, 270, 342, 348, 349, 352, 1174; Cox, *The March to the Sea—Franklin and Nashville* (New York, 1882), 86–87 (hereafter cited as *Franklin and Nashville*); and John K. Shellenberger, *The Battle of Franklin* (Cleveland, 1916), 13. Cox's description of the mid-day activities is from *Battle of Franklin*, 62–63. For the information on the Carter House and family during the battle, as well as the associated quotes from General Cox, consult the article by Dan M. Robison, "The Carter House: Focus of the Battle of Franklin," *Tennessee Historical Quarterly*, XXII (March 1963), 3–21. The observation of the soldier from the Twenty-sixth Ohio, as he watched the Confederate maneuvers, is taken from page 222 of "The Battle of Franklin," *Tennessee Historical Magazine*, VI (Oct. 1920), 213–65. The opinions of Cox and Stanley about the unexpectedness of the enemy attack are found in the former's *Battle of Franklin*, 68, and in the latter's report, *OR*, XLV, pt. 1, 115. The Weaver letter is in the *Franklin Review Appeal*, Nov. 27, 1880. The criticisms of Schofield are found in Shellenberger, *Battle of Franklin*, 39, 40, and in James B. Steedman, "Robbing the Dead," *New York Times*, June 22, 1881. For a defense of Schofield's actions see McDonough, *Schofield*, 121–22, and Cox, *Franklin and Nashville*, 87, as well as Cox, *Battle of Franklin*, 286. For initial events in Wagner's advanced brigades, see Shellenberger, *Battle of Franklin*, 14–17.

From the Confederate viewpoint, quoting Capers, see *OR*, XLV, pt. 1, 737.

For the desperate fighting as the Confederates penetrated the Union center near the Carter House, consult *OR*, XLV, pt. 1, 270–71, 393, 256, 737, 116, 352–54, 334, 379–80, 251, 240–41, 418, 720–21, 429–30, 714, 742–43; Shellenberger, *Battle of Franklin*, 20–28; Cox, *Franklin and Nashville*, 88–90, 97; Cox, *Battle of Franklin*, 118–19, 156–57, 200; W.A. Keesy, *War: As Viewed from the Ranks* (Norwalk, Ohio, 1898), 126–27; Norman D. Brown, ed., *One of Cleburne's Command: The Civil War Reminiscences and Diary of Captain Samuel T. Foster, Granbury's Texas Brigade, CSA* (Austin, Tex., 1980), 147–48; Sam R. Watkins, *"Co. Aytch," Maury Grays, First Tennessee Regiment; or A Side Show of the Big Show* (Jackson, Tenn., 1952), 218–21; Marshall P. Thatcher, *A Hundred Battles in the West, St. Louis to Atlanta, 1861–1865* (Detroit, 1884), 209; Hugh Walker, "Bloody Franklin," *Civil War Times Illustrated*, Special Nashville Edition (Dec. 1964), 23; Grady McWhiney and Perry D. Jamieson, *Attack and Die: Civil War Military Tactics and the Southern Heritage* (University, Ala. 1982), 15; "A Confederate's Recollections of the Battle of Franklin," *Civil War Times Illustrated*, Special Nashville Edition (Dec. 1964), 24.

CHAPTER 6

Much of the information in this chapter was obtained from the several dozen battle reports in *OR*, XLV, pt. I.

Additional information was obtained from numerous sources. One should consult Issac Shannon, "Sharpshooters with Hood's Army, "*CV*, XV (March 1907), 124–25, W.A. Washburn, "Cleburne's Division at Franklin," *CV*, XXIII (Jan. 1905), 27–28; Tilliam H. Stevens, " 'Other Side' in Battle of Franklin," *CV*, XI (April 1903), 166–67; James H. M'Neilly, "Franklin—Incidents of the Battle," *CV*, XXVI (Mach 1918), 117–18; "Confederate Monument at Franklin," *CV*, VIII (Jan. 1900), 6–9; "Another Union Veteran Writes of Franklin," *CV*, XI (April 1903); E. Shapard, "At Spring Hill and Franklin Again," *CV*, XXIV (March 1916), 138–39.

See also Hardin P. Figuers, "A Boy's Impressions of the Battle of Franklin," MS in Figures Memoir, Tennessee State Archives; Crownover, *Battle of Franklin*, 17–24; Park Marshall, "Artillery in the Battle of

Franklin," *CV*, XXIII (March 1915), 101' Buck, *Cleburne and His Command, 281–83; Purdue and Purdue, Pat Cleburne,* 421–26; Henry Stone, "Repelling Hood's Invasion of Tennessee," *Battles and Leaders of the Civil War* (4 vols., New York, 1956), 4:449–53.

CHAPTER 7

For Schofield's movements after the battle, consult the many battle reports in *OR*, XLV, pt. 1. For the cavalry operations see Henry, *"First With the Most" Forrest,* 396–400; James H. Wilson, "The Union Cavalry in the Hood Campaign," *Battles and Leaders of the Civil War,* IV, 466–67; John Allan Wyeth, *That Devil Forrest: a Life of General Nathan Bedford Forrest* (New York, 1959), 480–83; battle reports in *OR*, XLV, pt. 1.

For descriptions and estimates of battle casualties, see James M'Neilly, "Franklin—Incidents of the Battle," 117–18; "Confederate Monument at Franklin," 9; Shapard, "At Spring Hill and Franklin Again," 139; Connelly, *Autumn of Glory,* 506; Purdue and Purdue, *Pat Cleburne,* 430–33, 444–45; Buck, *Cleburne and His Command,* 284–93; Crownover, *Battle of Franklin,* 26–29.

For Hood's pursuit to Nashville and the ensuing defeat at the battle of Nashville, and retreat, see Hood, *Advance and Retreat,* 299–300; Hood to James Seddon, Dec. 5, 1864, in John Bell Hood Papers, Duke; Hood to Beauregard, Dec. 3, 1864, in Confederate Archives–Army of Tennessee; *OR* XLV, pt. 2, 628, 653, 659; Connelly, *Autumn of Glory,* 506–13; Horn, *Army of Tennessee,* 404–21; see also Stanley Horn, *The Decisive Battle of Nashville* (Baton Rouge, 1956), and Hay, *Hood's Tennessee Campaign.*

For the H.P. Figuers recollections see *CV*, XXIII (1915), 4–7. The young girl's recollections are also in *CV*, III (1895), 72–73. Dr. Roberts's account is in *Miller's Photographic History of the War,* VII, 256–58. For W.A. Keesy, consult *War: As Viewed from the Ranks,* 127.

EPILOGUE

For Thomas's position on the National Cemetery, see J.T. Trowbridge, *The South: A Tour of Its Battlefields and Ruined Cities* (Hartford,

Conn., 1866), 284. Also consulted were several letters to Mrs. N.B. Dozier, particularly Park Marshall to Mrs. Dozier, April 8, 1910 and G.W. Gordon (the former Confederate general, later a member of the U.S. House of Representatives) to Mrs. Dozier, Feb. 22, 1910. These letters are in the possession of Mr. Wade Bobo of Franklin, Tenn.

Information on the plans and work to make a movie about the battle may be found in Marshall Morgan's columns, "Here Today," *Nashville Tennessean*, Sept. 5, 12, 19, 1963. For information on Confederate reunions see various issues of *CV*.

# COMMENTARY ON SOURCES

This volume resulted from several years of independent research by the authors on the history of the Civil War in the western theater.

Such work obviously has required an examination of available manuscript sources. On the Confederate side, such documents are far-flung, but the Confederate Records Division, National Archives, is the touchstone of such research. Aside from the P.G.T. Beauregard and John Bell Hood papers, many other collections are helpful, such as Correspondence of the Western Department and the Army of the Mississippi, 1861–65; Letters, Orders and Circulars Sent and Received, Medical Director's Office, Army of Tennessee, 1862–65; Communications Received by Major General P.R. Cleburne's Division, 1862–64; Special Orders, Army of the Mississippi, Department No. 2 and Department and Army of Tennessee, 1862–64; Orders and Circulars, Army of Tennessee and Subordinate Commands, 1863–64; Miscellaneous Records, Army of Tennessee, 1863–65; and Letters Sent and Endorsements on Letters Received, Army of Tennessee, 1863–64. Such represent only a part of the vast number of official collections having some bearing on the Franklin tragedy.

These are only the beginning of a multitude of collections concerning the Army of Tennessee and the Franklin campaign of 1864. The Braxton Bragg Papers, Western Reserve Historical Society, provide background information on the western theater command problems of 1864. Other collections are important for understanding the command decision that brought Hood's army from Georgia to Middle Tennessee. One should consult the Jefferson Davis Papers, Duke Univ; John Bell Hood Papers, Nationl Archives; William J. Hardee Papers, Alabama State Department of Archives and History; P.G.T. Beauregard Letters, Univ. of Texas; P.G.T. Beauregard Papers, National Archives; P.G.T. Beauregard Papers, Library of Congress, and others.

Some of these collections provide also important material on Hood's march from Florence, Alabama, to Franklin in November 1864. In addition, one should consult the Charles Todd Quintard Diary, Univ. of the South; Wigfall Family Papers, Library of Congress; Campbell Brown

Reminiscences, Tennessee State Archives; Ezra Carman Papers, New York Public Library; Gale-Polk Papers, Southern Historical Collection, Univ. of North Carolina, and others.

Fewer actual manuscript sources are available for the battle itself, which is due in part to the high casualty rate among Confederate officers. There are some that provide important material regarding both the battle and its aftermath. One should consult Hardin P. Figuers, "A Boy's Impressions of the Battle of Franklin," ms. in Figuers Memoir, Tennessee State Archives; John Bell Hood Papers, Duke Univ.; Confederate Archives—Army of Tennessee Papers, Duke Univ.; John B. Lindsley Diary, Tennessee State Archives; Leonidas Polk Papers, Univ. of the South; John Bell Hood Papers, National Archives; Wigfall Family Papers, Library of Congress; and the Captain A.J. Brown Diary, Evans Memorial Library, Aberdeen, Miss.

For Union operations, the most important manuscript sources are the John M. Schofield Papers and the James H. Wilson Papers, Library of Congress. See also the James H. Wilson diaries, Delaware State Historical Society. Helpful as well are the George H. Thomas Papers and the William T. Sherman Papers, Library of Congress.

Obviously any listing of printed sources for the battle should begin with the *War of the Rebellion: A Compilation of the Official Records of the Union and Confederate Armies* (73 vols., Washington, D.C., 1880–1901). Due to the severe officer casualty rates at Franklin, the ensuing battle of Nashville, and the dissolution of the army, there are far fewer Confederate officer reports of Franklin than one finds for the Federal army.

One should consult the standard works on the Army of Tennessee. These include Thomas Connelly, *Army of the Heartland: The Army of Tennessee, 1861–1862* (Baton Rouge, 1967); Thomas Connelly, *Autumn of Glory: The Army of Tennessee, 1862–1865* (Baton Rouge, 1971); and Stanley Horn, *The Army of Tennessee* (Norman, Okla., 1955). A good documentary study of war in the western theater is provided by Stanley Horn, ed., *Tennessee's War, 1861–1865, Described by Participants* (Nashville, 1965). A brief overview of war in the West is provided by Thomas Connelly, *Civil War Tennessee* (Knoxville, 1979).

There are few monographs relating solely to either the Tennessee campaign of 1864 or the battle of Franklin. Thomas Robson Hay's *Hood's Tennessee Campaign* (New York, 1929) is the best older source for the operations that led both armies from Georgia to Middle Tennessee. The strength of this volume does not rest as much with the account of Franklin as in the detailed account of Hood's strategic maneuvers through Georgia and Alabama. Older but helpful accounts of Federal movements are found in Levi T. Schofield, *The Retreat from Pulaski to Nashville* (Cleveland, 1909), and Jacob D. Cox, *The March to the Sea—Franklin and Nashville* (New York, 1906).

A briefer but good account of Schofield's approach to Franklin is contained in Henry Stone, "Repelling Hood's Invasion of Tennessee," *Battles and Leaders of the Civil War* (4 vols., New York, 1956), 4: 440–64. Stone's article is also very helpful on the battle itself.

Accounts of cavalry maneuvers both before and during the battle are fairly extensive. General James Wilson's activities are chronicled in his memoir, *Under the Old Flag* (2 vols., New York, 1912), and in "The Union Cavalry in the Hood Campaign," *Battles and Leaders*, IV, 466–71. Both accounts are in part a defense of Wilson's activities from Columbia to Franklin.

Several biographies of General Nathan Bedford Forrest provide valuable material on both the campaign and the battle. Important are Robert Selph Henry, *"First with the Most" Forrest* (Indianapolis, 1944), and John Allan Wyeth, *That Devil Forrest: Life of General Nathan Bedford Forrest* (New York, 1959). Some other help is obtained from the much older Thomas Jordan and J.P. Pryor, *Campaigns of Lieut.-Gen. N.B. Forrest, and of Forrest's Cavalry* (New Orleans, 1868).

There are few books dealing solely with the battle of Franklin. General Jacob D. Cox's *The Battle of Franklin, Tennessee, November 30, 1864* (New York, 1897) is valuable for its observations on terrain and Union positions on the field. Robert Banks's brief *The Battle of Franklin* (New York, 1908) is of little assistance. A brief but very helpful modern study is a monograph reprint from the *Tennessee Historical Quarterly* with added maps, Sims Crownover, *The Battle of Franklin* (Nashville, 1955). Helpful also is Henry Stone's "The Battle of Franklin," in *Papers of the Military Historical Society of Massachusetts, Campaigns in Kentucky and Tennessee*, VII (Boston, 1908).

Biographies and reminiscences of commanders at Franklin are unfortunately meager. General John Bell Hood's memoir, *Advance and Retreat: Personal Experiences in the United States and Confederate States Armies* (Bloomington, Ind. 1959), must be used with caution; it is more a military apology than a memoir. Two older biographies of Hood provide some background material. John P. Dyer's *The Gallant Hood* (Indianapolis, 1950) is more useful than Richard O'Connor's *Hood: Cavalier General* (New York, 1949).

At the time this manuscript was submitted for publication, the best and most recent biography of Hood had not appeared—Richard M.

McMurry, *John Bell Hood and the War for Southern Independence* (Lexington, Ky., 1982). However, both authors had occasion to examine this work while it was in manuscript form.

General John McAllister Schofield's memoir, *Forty Six Years in the Army* (New York, 1897), must, like Hood's memoir, be used with caution, for it too has the marks of being an apology, although not in so pronounced a manner as the Confederate commander's. Compare it with James L. McDonough, *Schofield: Union General in the Civil war and Reconstruction* (Tallahassee, Fl., 1972).

Other scattered biographies and reminiscences provide some help. *Pat Cleburne: Confederate General*, by Howell and Elizabeth Purdue (Hillsboro, Tex., 1973) is a valuable source for the battle. Important as well is the well-known reminiscence by Cleburne's former staff officer, Irving A. Buck, titled *Cleburne and His Command*, ed. Thomas Robson Hay (Jackson, Tenn., 1959). Some assistance was provided by Park Marshall, *A Life of William B. Bate* (Nashville, 1908), and by Bromfield Ridley, ed., *Battles and Sketches of the Army of Tennessee* (Mexico, Mo., 1906).

Certain studies of General George Thomas add dimension to Schofield's movement into Middle Tennessee. These include Freeman Cleaves, *Rock of Chickamauga: The Life of General George H. Thomas* (Norman, Okla., 1948); Francis McKinney, *Education in Violence: The Life of George H. Thomas* (Detroit, 1961); Wilbur D. Thomas, *General George H. Thomas, the Indomitable Warrior* (New York, 1964); and Thomas V. Van Horn, *The Life of Major General George H. Thomas* (New York, 1882). Background material on Hood's maneuvers is found in T. Harry Williams, *P. G. T. Beauregard, Napoleon in Gray* (Baton Rouge, 1955), and Alfred Roman, *The Military Operations of General Beauregard in the War Between the States, 1861 to 1865* (2 vols., New York, 1883).

Although his corps had far less paricipation at Franklin, General Stephen D. Lee's movements were important and have been treated well in Herman Hattaway, *General Stephen D. Lee* (Jackson, Miss., 1976). Unfortunately, writings on the two main Confederate leaders, Generals Benjamin F. Cheatham and Alexander P. Stewart, are almost non-existent, save for scattered references in older periodicals such as the *Southern Historical Society Papers* and *Confederate Veteran*. Aside from Schofield and Wilson, Federal commanders have been largely neglected. General Jacob Cox's works previously cited are valuable, as is his memoir, *Military Reminiscences of the United States*. Scattered biographical information on some Union leaders is available in the voluminous volumes of the *Military Order of the Loyal Legion of the United States*. Some

Confederate biographical information is available in Clement Evans, ed., *Confederate Military History* (12 vols., Atlanta, 1899).

The reminiscences of private soldiers at Franklin are surprisingly few in number. A few are scattered through the many volumes of the *Confederate Veteran.* Some are contained in the numerous regimental histories of the Army of Tennessee, which are listed in the volumes by Thomas Connelly cited previously, *Army of the Heartland: The Army of Tennessee, 1861–1862* and *Autumn of Glory: The Army of Tennessee, 1862–1865.*

Useful biographical information on some officers who participated at Franklin may be obtained from studies of other battles on the western front. Glenn Tucker's *Chickamauga: Bloody Battle in the West* (New York, 1961) is useful. Consult also James L. McDonough, *Shiloh—In Hell Before Night* (Knoxville, 1977); James Pickett Jones, *Yankee Blitzkrieg: Wilson's raid through Alabama and Georgia* (Athens, Ga., 1976); James L. McDonough, *Stones River—Bloody Winter in Tennessee* (Knoxville, 1980); Wiley Sword, *Shiloh: Bloody April* (New York, 1974); and Stanley Horn, *The Decisive Battle of Nashville* (Baton Rouge, 1956). Horn's book is useful as well in chronicling the movements that brought Hood's and Schofield's armies from Georgia to Middle Tennessee.

Other books providing useful background on the Army of Tennessee include Grady McWhiney, *Braxton Bragg and Confederate Defeat* (New York, 1969); Charles P. Roland, *Albert Sidney Johnston: Soldier of Three Republics* (Austin, 1964); Nathaniel C. Hughes, Jr., *General William J. Hardee: Old Reliable* (Baton Rouge, 1965); and Joseph H. Parks, *General Leonidas Polk, C.S.A., The Fighting Bishop* (Baton Rouge, 1954).

Certain tactical and strategic studies of the larger war provide insight into the Franklin tragedy. A better understanding of Hood's violent assault tactics is garnered by reading Grady McWhiney and Perry D. Jamison, *Attack and Die: Civil War Military Tactics and the Southern Heritage* (University, Ala., 1982), as well as McWhiney's essay "Who Whipped Whom? Confederate Defeat Reexamined" in *Southerners and Other Americans* (New York, 1973).

For an overview of strategic and command policies that led Hood to the Franklin field, several works offer assistance. Overall Confederate strategy is analyzed in Thomas L. Connelly and Archer Jones, *The Politics of Command: Factions and Ideas in Confederate Strategy* (Baton Rouge, 1973). Although the title relates to an earlier period, much insight into the difficulties of the Confederate system of departmental command is provided by Archer Jones, *Confederate Strategy from Shiloh to Vicksburg*

(Baton Rouge, 1961). An overall understanding of the workings of Confederate command is obtained from Frank Vandiver, *Rebel Brass: The Confederate Command System* (Baton Rouge, 1956).

Topographic and geographic aids are important to an understanding of the Franklin battle and the entire campaign. Obviously the atlas accompanying *The War of the Rebellion: A Compilation of the Official Records* is essential. Equally important are the modern quadrangles issued by the United States Geological Survey. Other useful maps are included in works cited previously such as Jacob D. Cox, *The Battle of Franklin*, Sims Crownover, *The Battle of Franklin*, Howell and Elizabeth Purdue, *Pat Cleburne: Confederate General*, and Thomas R. Hay, *Hood's Tennessee Campaign*.

Certain special studies of the Spring Hill affair deserve mention. Readers should consult Stanley Horn, "The Spring Hill Legend—A Reappraisal," *Civil War Times*, VIII (April 1969), 20–32; W.T. Crawford, "The Mystery of Spring Hill," *Civil War History*, I (June, 1955), 101–26; John K. Shellenberger, "The Fighting at Spring Hill, Tenn.," *Confederate Veteran*, XXXVI (April 1928), 143; B.F. Cheatham, "The Lost Opportunity at Spring Hill—General Cheatham's Reply to General Hood, *"Southern Historical Society Papers*, IX (1881), 524–25; J.P. Young, "Hood's Failure at Spring Hill," *Confederate Veteran*, XVI (Jan. 1908), 27–31; and Arthur Noll, ed., *Doctor Quintard, Chaplain C.S.A. and Second Bishop of Tennessee; Being His Story of the War (1861–1865)* (Sewanee, Tenn., 1905). A synthesis of conflicting accounts of the Spring Hill matter is provided in James L. McDonough, "West Point Classmates—Eleven Years Later: Some Observations on the Spring Hill-Franklin Campaign," *Tennessee Historical Quarterly*, XXVIII (Summer 1969), 182–196. Also see James L. McDonough, "John McAllister Schofield," *Civil War Times Illustrated*, XIII (Aug. 1974), 10–17, which relates in part to the Spring Hill affair. Another helpful article is Campbell H. Brown, "To Rescue the Confederacy," *Civil War Times Illustrated*, Special Nashville Campaign Edition (Dec. 1964), 13–15, 44–48.

# Organization of the Infantry of the
# CONFEDERATE ARMY
*In the Middle Tennessee Campaign*
*November 1864*

## ARMY OF TENNESSEE
Lieutenant General John Bell Hood, Commanding

### Cheatham's Corps
Major General Benjamin F. Cheatham

#### Cleburne's division
Major General Patrick Cleburne

*Govan's Brigade*
Brig. Gen. Daniel C. Govan

First Arkansas
Second Arkansas
Fifth Arkansas
Sixth Arkansas
Seventh Arkansas
Eighth Arkansas
Thirteenth Arkansas
Fifteenth Arkansas
Nineteenth Arkansas
Twenty-fourth Arkansas

*Granbury's Brigade*
Brig. Gen. Hiram B. Granbury

Thirty-fifth Tennessee
Sixth Texas
Seventh Texas

Tenth Texas
Fifteenth Texas
Seventeenth Texas Cavalry (dismounted)
Eighteenth Texas Cavalry (dismounted)
Twenty-fourth Texas Cavalry (dismounted)
Twenty-fifth Texas Cavalry (dismounted)

*Lowrey's Brigade*
Brig. Gen. Mark B. Lowrey
Sixteenth Alabama
Thirty-third Alabama
Forty-fifth Alabama
Eighth Mississippi
Thirty-second Mississippi
Third Mississippi Battalion
Fifth Mississippi Battalion

BROWN'S DIVISION
Major General John C. Brown

*Gist's Brigade*
Brig. Gen. States Rights Gist

Forty-sixth Georgia
Sixty-fifth Georgia
Sixteenth South Carolina
Twenty-fourth South Carolina

*Maney's Brigade*
Brig. Gen. John C. Carter

First Tennessee
Fourth Tennessee
Sixth Tennessee
Eighth Tennessee
Ninth Tennessee
Sixteenth Tennessee
Twenty-seventh Tennessee
Twenty-eighth Tennessee
Fiftieth Tennessee

*Strahl's Brigade*
Brig. Gen. Otho F. Strahl

Fourth Tennessee
Fifth Tennessee
Nineteenth Tennessee
Twenty-fourth Tennessee
Thirty-first Tennessee
Thirty-third Tennessee
Thirty-eighth Tennessee
Forty-first Tennessee

*Vaughan's Brigade*
Brig. Gen. George W. Gordon
Eleventh Tennessee
Twelfth Tennessee
Thirteenth Tennessee
Twenty-ninth Tennessee
Forty-seventh Tennessee
Fifty-first Tennessee
Fifty-second Tennessee
One Hundred and Fifty-fourth Tennessee

BATE'S DIVISION
## Major General William B. Bate

*Finley's Brigade*
Colonel Robert Bullock

First Florida
Third Florida
Fourth Florida
Sixth Florida
Seventh Florida
First Florida Cavalry (dismounted)

*Jackson's Brigade*
Brig. Gen. Henry R. Jackson

First Georgia
Twenty-fifth Georgia

Twenty-ninth Georgia
Thirtieth Georgia
Sixty-sixth Georgia
First Georgia Sharpshooters

*Tyler's Brigade*
Brig. Gen. Thomas Benton Smith

Second Tennessee
Tenth Tennessee
Twentieth Tennessee
Thirty-seventh Tennessee
Thirty-seventh Georgia
Fourth Georgia Sharpshooters

STEWART'S CORPS
Lieutenant General Alexander P. Stewart

FRENCH'S DIVISION
Major General Samuel G. French

*Ector's Brigade*
Brig. Gen. M.D. Ector

Twenth-ninth North Carolina
Thirty-ninth North Carolina
Ninth Texas
Tenth Texas Cavalry (dismounted)
Fourteenth Texas Cavalry (dismounted)
Thirty-second Texas Cavalry (dismounted)

*Cockrell's Brigade*
Brig. Gen. Francis M. Cockrell

*(Regiments unknown)*

*Sears's Brigade*
Brig. Gen. Claudius Sears

Fourth Mississippi
Thirty-fifth Mississippi

Thirty-sixth Mississippi
Thirty-ninth Mississippi
Forty-sixth Mississippi

LORING'S DIVISION
## Major General William Wing Loring

*Adams's Brigade*
Brig. Gen. John Adams

Sixth Mississippi
Fourteenth Mississippi
Fifteenth Mississippi
Twentieth Mississippi
Twenty-third Mississippi
Forty-third Mississippi

*Featherston's Brigade*
Brig. Gen. Winfield S. Featherston

First Mississippi
Third Mississippi
Twenty-second Mississippi
Thirty-first Mississippi
Thirty-third Mississippi
Fortieth Mississippi
First Mississippi Battalion

*Scott's Brigade*
Brig. Gen. Thomas M. Scott

Twenty-seventh Alabama
Thirty-fifth Alabama
Forty-ninth Alabama
Fifty-fifth Alabama
Fifty-seventh Alabama
Twelfth Louisiana

WALTHALL'S DIVISION
## Major General Edward C. Walthall

*Quarles's Brigade*
Brig. Gen. William A. Quarles

First Alabama
Forty-second Tennessee
Forty-sixth Tennessee
Forty-eighth Tennessee
Forty-ninth Tennessee
Fifty-third Tennessee
Fifty-fifth Tennessee

*Reynolds's Brigade*
Brig. Gen. Daniel H. Reynolds

Fourth Arkansas
Ninth Arkansas
Twenty-fifth Arkansas

*Cantey's Brigade*
Brig. Gen. Charles M. Shelley

Seventeenth Alabama
Twenty-sixth Alabama
Twenth-ninth Alabama
Thirty-seventh Mississippi

LEE'S CORPS
Lieutenant General Stephen Dill Lee

JOHNSON'S DIVISION
Major General Edward Johnson
*Brantley's Brigade*
Brig. Gen. William Brantley

Twenty-fourth Mississippi
Twenty-seventh Mississippi
Thirtieth Mississippi
Thirty-fourth Mississippi

*Deas' Brigade*
Brig. Gen. Zachariah C. Deas

Nineteenth Alabama
Twenty-second Alabama
Twenty-fifth Alabama
Thirty-ninth Alabama
Fiftieth Alabama

*Manigault's Brigade*
Brig. Gen. Arthur M. Manigault

Twenty-fourth Alabama
Twenty-eighth Alabama
Thirty-fourth Alabama
Tenth South Carolina
Nineteenth South Carolina

*Sharp's Brigade*
Brig. Gen. Jacob H. Sharp

Seventh Mississippi
Ninth Mississippi
Tenth Mississippi
Forty-first Mississippi
Forty-fourth Mississippi

*Cantey's Brigade*
(Commander Unknown)

Seventh Alabama
Twenty-sixth Alabama
Twenty-ninth Alabama
Thirty-seventh Mississippi

STEVENSON'S DIVISION
Maj. Gen. Carter L. Stevenson

*Pettus's Brigade*
Brig. Gen. Edmund W. Pettus

Twentieth Alabama Regiment
Twenty-third Alabama Regiment

Thirtieth Alabama Regiment
Thirty-first Alabama Regiment
Forty-sixth Alabama Regiment

*Cumming's Brigade*
Col. Elihu P. Watkins

Thirty-fourth Georgia Regiment
Thirty-sixth Georgia Regiment
Thirty-ninth Georgia Regiment
Fifty-sixth Georgia Regiment

CLAYTON'S DIVISION
Maj. Gen. Henry D. Clayton

*Gibson's Brigade*
Brig. Gen. Randall L. Gibson

First Louisiana Regiment
Fourth Louisiana Regiment
Thirteenth Louisiana Regiment
Sixteenth Louisiana Regiment
Nineteenth Louisiana Regiment
Twentieth Louisiana Regiment
Thirtieth Louisiana Regiment

*Stovall's Brigade*
Brig. Gen. Marcellus A. Stovall

Fortieth Georgia Regiment
Forty-first Georgia Regiment
Forty-second Georgia Regiment
Forty-third Georgia Regiment
Fifty-second Georgia Regiment

*Holtzclaw's Brigade*
Brig. Gen. James Holtzclaw

Eighteenth Alabama Regiment
Thirty-second Alabama Regiment
Thirty-sixth Alabama Regiment
Thirty-eighth Alabama Regiment
Fifty-eighth Alabama Regiment

# Organization of the Infantry of the

# FEDERAL ARMY

*In the Middle Tennessee Campaign*

*November 1864*

Major General John McAllister Schofield, Commanding

FOURTH ARMY CORPS

Brigadier General David Stanley

FIRST DIVISION

Brigadier General Nathan Kimball

*First Brigade*

Colonel Isaac M. Kirby

Twenty-first Illinois
Thirty-eighth Illinois
Thirty-first Indiana
One Hundred and first Ohio

*Second Brigade*

Brigadier General Walter C. Whitaker

Ninety-sixth Illinois
Thirty-fifth Indiana
Twenty-first Kentucky
Twenty-third Kentucky
Fortieth Ohio
Forty-fifth Ohio
Fifty-first Ohio

*Third Brigade*
Brigadier General William Grose

Seventy-fifth Illinois
Eightieth Illinois
Eighty-fourth Illinois
Ninth Indiana
Thirtieth Indiana
Eighty-fourth Indiana
Seventy-seventh Pennsylvania

### SECOND DIVISION
## Brigadier General George D. Wagner

*First Brigade*
Colonel Emerson E. Opdycke

Thirty-sixth Illinois
Forty-fourth Illinois
Seventy-third Illinois
Seventy-fourth Illinois
Eighty-eighth Illinois
One Hundred and Twenty-fifth Ohio
Twenty-fourth Wisconsin

*Second Brigade*
Colonel John Q. Lane

One Hundredth Illinois
Fortieth Indiana
Fifty-seventh Indiana
Twenty-eighth Kentucky
Twenty-sixth Ohio
Ninety-seventh Ohio

*Third Brigade*
Colonel Joseph Conrad

Forty-second Illinois
Fifty-first Illinois
Seventy-ninth Illinois

Fifteenth Missouri
Sixty-fourth Ohio
Sixty-fifth Ohio

### THIRD DIVISION
## Brigadier General Thomas J. Wood

*First Brigade*
Colonel Abel D. Streight

Eighty-ninth Illinois
Fifty-first Indiana
Eighth Kansas
Fifteenth Ohio
Forty-ninth Ohio

*Second Brigade*
Colonel P. Sidney Post

Fifty-ninth Illinois
Forty-first Ohio
Seventy-first Ohio
Ninety-third Ohio
One Hundred and Twenty-fourth Ohio

*Third Brigade*
Colonel Frederick Knefler

Seventy-ninth Indiana
Eighty-sixth Indiana
Thirteenth Ohio
Nineteenth Ohio

### TWENTY-THIRD ARMY CORPS
## Major General John McAllister Schofield

### SECOND DIVISION
## Major General Thomas H. Ruger

*First Brigade*
Brigadier General Joseph A. Cooper

One Hundred and Thirtieth Indiana
Twenty-sixth Kentucky
Twenty-fifth Michigan
Ninety-ninth Ohio
Third Tennessee
Sixth Tennessee

*Second Brigade*
Colonel Orlando H. Moore

One Hundred and seventh Illinois
Eightieth Indiana
One Hundred and Twenty-ninth Indiana
Twenty-third Michigan
One Hundred and Eleventh Ohio
One Hundred and Eighteenth Ohio

*Third Brigade*
Colonel Silas A. Strickland

Ninety-first Indiana
Seventy-second Illinois
Fiftieth Ohio
Forty-fourth Missouri
One Hundred and Eighty-third Ohio

THIRD DIVISION
Brigadier General Jacob Dolson Cox

*First Brigade*
Brigadier General James W. Reilly

Twelfth Kentucky
Sixteenth Kentucky
One Hundredth Ohio
One Hundred and Fourth Ohio
Eighth Tennessee

[ 211

*Second Brigade*
Colonel John S. Casement

Sixty-fifth Illinois
Sixty-fifth Indiana
One Hundred and Twenty-fourth Indiana
One Hundred and Third Ohio
Fifth Tennessee

*Third Brigade*
Colonel Israel N. Stiles

One Hundred and Twelfth Illinois
Sixty-third Indiana
One Hundred and Twentieth Indiana
One Hundred and Twenty-eighth Indiana

# INDEX

[ 213

*Five Tragic Hours* was composed on the Mergenthaler Linotron 202N Phototypesetter in eleven point Bembo, one-point line spacing. The book was designed by Guy Fleming, composed by Williams, Chattanooga, Tennessee, printed by offset lithography at Thomson-Shore, Inc., Dexter, Michigan, and bound by John H. Dekker & Sons, Grand Rapids, Michigan. The paper on which the book is printed is designed for an effective life of at least three hundred years.

THE UNIVERSITY OF TENNESSEE PRESS : KNOXVILLE